Medicine

Medicine Balls II

– the *other* one

Dr Rob Buckman

Cartoons by
Colin Wheeler

PAPERMAC

First published in paperback 1988 by
PAPERMAC
a division of Macmillan Publishers Limited
4 Little Essex Street London WC2R 3LF
and Basingstoke

Associated companies in Auckland, Delhi, Dublin, Gaborone, Hamburg, Harare, Hong Kong, Johannesburg, Kuala Lumpur, Lagos, Manzini, Melbourne, Mexico City, Nairobi, New York, Singapore, and Tokyo

The illustration on page 114 reproduced by permission of *Punch* December 1986

ISBN 0-333-48283-2

Typeset by Rowland Phototypesetting Limited
Bury St Edmunds, Suffolk
Printed in Hong Kong

Contents

Introduction

Hello and welcome to this important epoch-making book.

There can be no doubt that we live in an age of Health Consciousness. Why, only last week a survey showed that at any one time 86 per cent of us are healthy and 71 per cent of us are conscious. Though rarely at the same time. But even so, health is something that concerns us all as a society, for under the skin are we not all fellow human beings, co-tenants of this frail planet and neighbours in the out-patient queue? Yes we are, particularly in Britain. Now I do not wish to stir controversy and inflame passions about the state of our health service. But in my view there is no doubt that, as regards spending on the National Health Service, no previous government in the whole history of this great country of ours has ever invested so much time and manpower in showing that no previous government in the whole history of this country of ours has ever invested so much time and manpower in the National Health Service. Of which I am one. Manpower I mean.

But of course, I am more than a mere cog or pawn in the vast puppet of the NHS. As an immensely famous and distinguished doctor and broadcaster, I feel that I have a role and responsibility as a leader and shaper of social attitudes. I could be wrong, but it so happens that I'm not. And it is in that role and with that responsibility that I now release this eagerly awaited collection of my writings which have never before been published except when they came out in *Punch* every week.

In this slim (but inexpensive) volume, you will find many answers to the questions you didn't even realise you wanted answered. Or asked. On matters of social controversy, public concern and rising hysteria, I speak out with a unique combination of common sense, clarity and authority. And sometimes I get it right as well. Where you have anxieties, I dispel them; where there is darkness, I illuminate; where there is ignorance and error, I dispense science and error; where there are misconceptions, I unmisconceive them.

Many people have marvelled at my consistent ability to identify and deal with the crucial health issues of our times. Perhaps I am being too modest when I say that if I cannot correctly identify the greatest health concerns of our age, then I cause them. Between these covers, you will find out how. And of course, it is between the covers that most of our health panics begin – in this book you will find that I deal unflinchingly and quite outspokenly with the thorny and difficult areas of thing. You know, stuff that goes wrong with your downbelows.

But why delay the inevitable? An introduction can only achieve so much, most of it to do with introducing. Some of you, wisely, may already have stopped reading the introduction after the first paragraph, leapt ahead to read the rest of the book and then returned to finish off this page, in which case welcome back and I hope you enjoyed the book. Some of you are probably still on the second paragraph, in which case I'll wait here until you're ready.

But for the rest of you, I hope that you will find what you read in this volume both educating and stimulating, nourishing and nurturing, intriguing and inveigling, edifying and terrifying.

Good luck and wash your hands after each chapter.

Dr Robert Buckman
Monaco – Mustique – Basingstoke

Sexology

As Britain's most famous and foremost doctor and broadcaster, I am often asked to handle very sensitive areas such as sex, particularly at times of increasing public anxiety and panic, e.g. if Claire Rayner is on holiday. In this chapter I survey thoroughly all the major aspects of sex, sexual physiology and fertility, except foreplay which I didn't have time for. Let us start then, as sexuality does, at puberty.

PUBERTY

Perhaps many of us think only of the outward manifestations of puberty including the changes in secondary sexual characteristics such as the shape of the hips, the breasts and so on. But puberty is much more than that, particularly to males. It is an awkward transition between youth and adulthood which so few of us traverse smoothly. In either direction.

Physiologically speaking, puberty is a time of very great changes of which the most noticeable are those of the body shape, the breasts (see above) and the pubic regions (see below – but don't stare). At the University of Southern California, a group of six eminent endocrinologists spent nearly four years studying the adolescent development of normal healthy youngsters (until they were caught) and many of their observations are of great importance in understanding not only the wider implications of the endocrine control of somatic growth, but also the workings of the American judicial system. Basically, the scientists measured over ninety different parameters of biological, metabolic, psychological, sexual and social functioning and found that the greatest rates of growth occurred in the teenagers' muscle bulk, glycogen stores, subcutaneous fat, vernacular and pocket money. These findings suggested that there existed a hormonal 'signal' which triggered growth in all these areas virtually simultaneously. The identification of this signal was exceptionally complex and is still only partly understood. But most scientists now believe puberty is started by a complex glycoprotein called luteinising-hormone-releasing-factor, though other scientists blame it on Brooke Shields. Perhaps one can best consider this complex topic under two headings – the physical effects of puberty, and the psycho-social effects of those physical effects (including consumer's rights). As regards the psychological effects of puberty, the definitive studies are undoubtedly those of the Yale group. The Yale sociologists Lofgren, Rizzetto, Nishioko and Bumm surveyed two thousand American teenagers and from their detailed findings concluded that two major kinds of problems could be identified. These they attributed to (a) the onset of puberty, or (b) the failure of onset of puberty. In Yale, at this point in time (summer of 1971), much of the American pubertal social culture was centred around the car or automobile, particularly the back seat. The findings of the Yale group suggested that the *rate* of psychological adjustment to puberty depended on three factors: parental pressure, peer-group pressure and – significantly – tyre-pressure. It is no coincidence that many of the great sociologists of the early Seventies have since gone on to achieve further eminence as garage mechanics.

Beards

Beards are not just a facial adornment but are an entire subculture in themselves. Perhaps. Like breasts, they are an outward manifestation that a young person has become a fully-grown man. No, that can't be right, but anyway, beards are recognised as badges of the full-grown male, not just in humans but in many other species that possess sophisticated social organisations e.g. clams. In many, pre-literate, hierarchical societies (e.g. Luton) the right to 'wear' a beard is one which does not come naturally, but which has to be

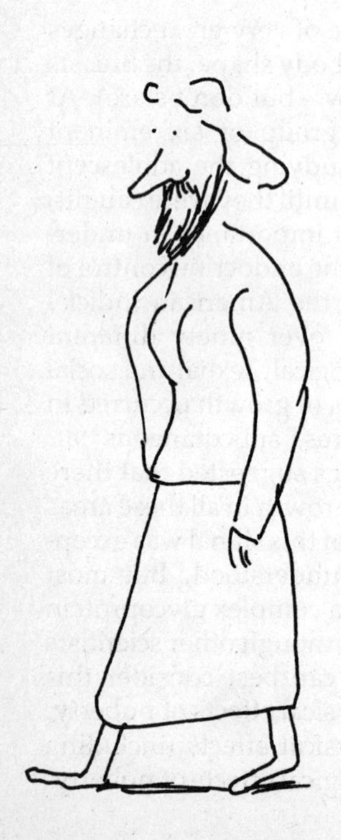

earned, often by means of an arduous and apparently meaningless ritual, such as darts. Some psychologists have identified certain groups of people as particularly 'beard-prone'. In these people, the beard serves as a 'psychological cosmetic' and is used by the person to disguise an obvious or even latent weakness or defect, for instance a weak chin, an overbearing mother or a particularly soiled shirt-front. From their in-depth studies on hundreds of young television personalities such as myself who have recently grown beards, the Metropolitan Police have concluded that a beard changes many aspects of a person's life. It not only enhances one's image of one's own virility and maturity, but forces one to adopt an entirely different attitude to eating spaghetti and blowing one's nose. Both of which may take up an entire afternoon and require hours of grooming, sometimes with a battery-driven vacuum-cleaner, if deleterious effects on one's social buoyancy, ego and sensuality are to be avoided. One wonders how Bluebeard did so well really, though maybe he never ate spaghetti or had a cold.

Breasts

Breasts pose a real problem. The point about breasts is that in our primitive ancestors they represented an extremely important part of the sexual signalling system, and were a means of transmitting a great deal of information about the bearer. They still do the same thing to this very day, which is not really a problem at all – in fact, I can't actually remember what the problem is. Maybe it was something to do with equality, which in breasts is a very desirable feature, generally speaking. As a matter of fact, the upper chest in both men and women is part of the so-called 'blush' area, and some scientists believe that breasts evolved as a means of amplifying this signal. In many parts of Australia, on the other hand, it is widely believed that breasts evolved as a means of selling newspapers. Either way, our response to a bosom is certainly one of the features of our behaviour that we have in common with the anthropoid apes, though there are of course very many important differences. For instance, many species including the orang-utan find *The Sun* an insufficient challenge to their intellect.

Pubic Hair

Pubic hair is another very difficult area. By definition, of course, pubic hair is that which grows in what is known as the erroneous zones, and since they grow only at the time of puberty, we know that they must require hormones in order to develop. However, what we don't know is how any particular hair 'knows' that it is destined to be a pubic hair, and why it is that pubic hair doesn't grow on your eyebrows or other unsuitable places. Of course, there are more aspects than hormonal-sensitivity, and it is perhaps a testament to the strength of the sexual signal of pubic hair that so much legal wrangling has surrounded its display. This culminated in the ruling of Oregon's Chief Justice, Shellac, who ruled that pubic hairs could be displayed provided there were no more than three of them, and they weren't moving. However, to return to the biology of the subject, perhaps the most important work on the nature of the pubic hair came from the pioneering work of the Oxford microbiologists, Bourne and Hollingsworth, who took single pubic hairs and, using a cryostatically-cooled microtome, produced ultra-thin sections. Examining these after tungsten counterstaining under an electron microscope, they proved conclusively that sections of pubic hair less than 10 micrometres thick are not in the least bit erotic.

THE DOCTOR ANSWERS YOUR QUESTIONS

Q: What are 'hives' and can you catch them from people?

A: 'Hives' is the name that we doctors use to describe the houses that bees live in, and you cannot catch them from people, you have to buy them.

SEXUAL DIFFERENTIATION

Few of us actually realise what it is that sets men apart from women. Some believe that it is simply signs on toilet doors, but that is incorrect. The answer is sexual differentiation, the mysterious process that causes a foetus to 'decide' whether to develop into a male or a female or anything in between, e.g. people in advertising. Here are the facts.

Gonads

I wonder if you know what **gonads** are? No, you're wrong. Actually, they are not the areas under both bits of the bikini, nor are they just those lower bits (the ones that used to be airbrushed out in *Health and Efficiency*). Those are not the gonads at all, those are the complex areas known as the **downbelows**, or, in common parlance, the 'secondary sexual characteristics', though to be frank they've always seemed damned primary to me.

Anyway, those bits are not the gonads. Or not all of them are the gonads. In the female, the gonads are actually the ovaries as a matter of fact, and on the male, they are the, you know, the oh, come on, you know perfectly well what they are, oh, all right, the goolies. Right, now can we get on?

Well now, surprising as it may seem, it is the gonads that actually turn us into either men or women, and not the colour of our bootees or the thoroughness of our toilet-training etc. Our sexual identity is determined initially by the nature of our gonadal development at a comparatively early stage in our embryonic life, usually about lunchtime on the second day. From then on, we remain – for the most part – the same sex as our gonads, rough hew them how we may (actually I was at school with a bloke called Rough Hugh and interestingly he now dresses in women's clothes, which has always bothered me – although more than it bothers him, apparently).

Anyway, there we are in the womb on the second or third day after fertilisation and in a bit of a rush if we're going to get our tracheal buds out by the second week and have our yolk-sac and amniotic membranes looking nice for the spring. And, on top of everything else, we've got to decide whether we're a bloke or a blokess.

Now, what I am going to say will surprise you – and me, come to that, so let's find out more together. Well, the plain fact is that human beings are basically female and require an additional signal to turn them into males. It's almost as if the female was the basic model, with the male being the one with the optional extras. But what is so interesting is that the nature of your gonads (and mine) is decided by things called sex chromosomes, which are code-named X and Y to avoid litigation against them.

As I've told you before, females have two X chromosomes and males have one X and one Y. Now, what happens to us on this fateful second or third day is that we sit there waiting to hear if we've got a Y chromosome – if we have, then we go ahead and develop testes, and all the hormonal *sequelae*, e.g. chest with extra holes for hairs, high blood-pressure, desire to play golf etc. If, on the other hand, we hear nothing at all in the way of a Y chromosome signalling to us, we simply go ahead with Plan A and turn into a female, develop ovaries and an ability to run the world by controlling those silly enough to listen to their Y chromosomes.

As any male chauvinist should realise by now, ours not to reason Y.

Endocrine Gender

However, sex doesn't just stop with the chromosomes (unless you're married of course). What happens next is that two bits of rather nondescript gristle which start off up near your flanks somewhere respond to the call of the chromosomes and turn into ovaries, or things – goolies. Whichever it is. I mean, they are.

Now, if ovaries are the order of the day, then they just sort of settle back and shift down a couple of inches and wait for the rest of the body to grow up round them, whereas if they are to become testes they begin a perilous journey out of the abdomen, through the nascent inguinal canal and into an area that will eventually be, embryologically speaking, in close proximity to the trouser-pocket. Now, the nature of that fraught migration has been explained to me dozens of times – actually, it even came up as an essay question in three of my exams. And I failed only twice so I must know something about it, but for the life of me I can't remember how it (or rather they) do it. I think perhaps they simply migrate towards magnetic south, except that might mean that the Australians could end up with their goolies in their brains (which some of them undoubtedly do – that being the only rational explanation for much of their behaviour, in my opinion).

Anyway, we're getting away from the point – in fact, so far away that we're getting quite close to another point altogether. Well, whatever happens to the gonadal streaks (as they are called at this tender stage in their ontogeny) they settle down comfortably in their new home and do absolutely sod all for about 14 years. Then they wake up suddenly overnight (or in another 11 years in my case) and ruin your life by giving you acne, and hair and gawkiness and Urges.

The precise nature of these Urges is what I shall deal with in the next section. If I feel like it.

Gender Identity

As Shakespeare once aptly put it, 'the apparel oft proclaimeth the man.' He might well have said 'the man and the woman' and he'd still have been wrong. And that's not just because it's so difficult to tell these days, what with the drugs and long hair etc etc, bring back the birch, national service, hanging and Oliver Cromwell. No, it's nothing to do with that – it's simply that what the apparel oft proclaimeth is the gender identity, which is to say the gender to which we would like to be perceived to belong.

This is where the full gamut of psycho-social factors comes into play – and work. Because our gender identity does not depend merely on the internal hormonal *milieu*, nor on the colour of the bootees in which our infant feet are first cosseted, nor on the strictness of our mother's toilet-training, our desire to get into Roedean, or any other variable. It seems to be inherent, in that some persons may be chromosomally, gonadally and hormonally one sex, and yet identify totally with the other. Interestingly, most endocrinologists do not consider this a 'disease' state. They would not call a burly man who wished to dress and identify himself as a woman 'ill' or 'sick', though they might have second thoughts if he decided to cross-dress as a pathological specimen, e.g. Madame Defarge, Joan Rivers or Edwina Currie. In fact, most endocrinologists seem to have second thoughts about anyone who dresses as Edwina Currie, particularly Edwina Currie.

THE DOCTOR ANSWERS YOUR QUESTIONS HONESTLY

Q: Have you been wearing my dress again?

A: No, dear, just the hat.

KISSING

As we move on to consider the physiology of sexual behaviour, I shall start with kissing (as all gentlemen should). This fascinating sexual ritual is little understood even by psycho-social behavioural scientists, who, as a group, are generally lousy at kissing.

Physical Aspects of Kissing

Kissing is one of the most fascinating things that human beings do (the other is the other) and what makes it so fascinating is that it has physical, hormonal, psychological, emotional and symbolic parameters. Plus the possibility that, within a long-term relationship like a marriage, your wife might catch you at it.

What actually happens when we kiss? Well, there are two major components to the process of kissing. The first is a mouth and the second is a something else. And it is the physical nature of that something else that creates the emotional context of the kiss as a transaction. Thus, the kissed object may be a kissee's mouth (affectionate) or cheek (French), the air (symbolic), a baby's head (maternal or perfunctory, e.g. during an election), a prelate's hand (devotional) or the boss's backside (expedient).

But what makes a kiss such a sensitive action is the fact that it employs the lips, and really can't be done without them, or at the very least one of them. Now lips are biologically speaking an example of muco-cutaneous junctions which is where mucous membranes join on to skin. Actually, it's quite difficult for a well-trained scientist to explain to a lay audience precisely what mucous membranes are, so I'll just say that among all membranes the mucous ones are my favourite, and leave it at that. But where they join on to real skin, they create a highly sensitive area often wrongly called 'an erroneous zone'.

Now such areas, including the lips, carry a very high number of sensory-receptors per square inch, have direct connections with the autonomic nervous system and autocrine release of neuro-humoral factors and are also good for inter-personal display mechanisms, e.g. lipstick. That is to say that they are specifically designed for sensitive physical contact with the outside world in order to relay precious information of vital importance to the brain, e.g. whether she still loves you, whether your soup's too hot, etc.

So, granted that the lips are such sensitive organs, what we do when we kiss them is to contract a muscle called the orbicularis oris which performs an action known in strictly anatomical terms as 'puckering up'. Once puckered up, the now corrugated lips are pressed against the other object, usually with reflex closure of the eyes (unless you've lost that loving feeling and it's gone gone gone, in which case they stay open).

At the moment of contact a large variety of psycho-endocrine phenomena may occur, including dramatic increase in parasympathetic tone (causing butterflies in the stomach), precipitate release of catecholamines (causing pounding of the heart), unexpected return of her husband (causing pounding of the head and a discussion that all the neighbours can hear), or hormonally-mediated cyclo-thymic melancholia, which is a deeply felt sense of confusion and dismay (e.g. on opening your eyes and seeing it's Zsa-Zsa Gabor).

The Evolution of Kissing

We are, of course, not the only animal species that kisses. Many of the primate apes can kiss, and some of them kiss each other (it's dirty work but somebody's got to do it). Lower vertebrates also kiss, e.g. humming birds, dogfish, Barbie dolls, snapdragons etc, but we are the only species that kiss in the back rows of cinemas instead of watching the film.

What is fascinating is that not all cultures use the kiss as greeting and erotic overture. For instance, the Eskimos don't kiss at all but rub noses, which doesn't sound half as much fun as kissing but has the significant advantage that you don't have to worry if you've been eating garlic. There is some evidence to suggest that a kiss was originally a signal of peaceful intentions. The Berlin anthropologists Hoeklein and Sinkë have proved (to their own satisfaction) that Cro-Magnon man used to kiss to demonstrate that he was not carrying weapons and could approach safely. Fossil evidence shows that in this way he was able to produce certain behavioural patterns in Cro-Magnon woman, e.g. coming back to his place, meeting his mum and dad (i.e. Neanderthal woman and a sophisticated orang-utan), cooking the dinner, producing a new species etc.

Even more controversially, the Kyoto palaeontologists Yin, Yang and Goldberg believe that dinosaurs used to kiss too, and were wiped out by an extraordinarily virulent type of dental caries. Whether or not this could have been prevented by putting fluoride into the primaeval swamps is a matter of some debate.

The Psychology of Kissing

Ah yes, the psychology of kissing! Breathes there a man with soul so dead (Shakespeare) that doesn't think he knows all about the psychology of kissing? No, there doesn't. A kiss, you see, is a surrender – be it ever so temporary and fleeting (which, with my luck, it usually is). A kiss is an oasis of verbal peace and silence, a gesture of suspended hostilities, a brief encounter of the oral kind, an ambiguous promise, and a motive force, a rationale, a *raison d'être* for important changes in your life (including getting rid of your chewing-gum).

We kiss our spouses, our lovers, our parents, our children, our pets, our hands; other people's spouses, lovers and pets, and the tarmac of other people's airports. And each kiss is different – a unique blend of grace, favour, respect and erotic arousal (a major problem if it's tarmac or someone else's pet). In fact, a kiss is a microcosm of all human frailty and magnificence and if there's one thing that we scientists can prove beyond any doubt it is that a kiss is still a kiss as time goes by. The trouble is we can't seem to stop the time going by. More research is clearly needed here.

THE DOCTOR RECALLS THE PAST

Q: Doctor, I've taken all my clothes off – where shall I put them?

A: Over there. On top of mine.

PARENTING

A consideration of the subject of kissing opens up several major areas of discussion, e.g. your place or mine, etc. And inevitably one comes on to the important topic of parenting. If one is not careful. Here are some exceptionally important observations on the subject.

Parenthood

When you come to think about it, parents are fascinating people (except to their children, of course). In fact, when it comes to keeping the species going, parents are one of the most important factors. The other important factor being children.

It is thus no coincidence that in order to ensure the survival of the human race, nature has made the desire to procreate a very deeply ingrained motivational drive. Particularly in California. Actually, in modern man, the desire to have children is the fourth most powerful human drive – the third most powerful being the desire not to have children. And the first two being hunger and the desire to watch football.

Anyway, the bond between parent and child is a powerful and complex one, comprising both 'nature and nurture'. Which means that the children inherit some things genetically from their parents (e.g. blue eyes, Throne of England etc) and some things they pick up from their parents as they go along (e.g. table manners, pocket-money, scabies etc).

It's worth remembering that inheritance is a two-way process and there are certain things that parents can inherit from their children – madness, for instance. Anyway, parents can undoubtedly exert a very deep and lasting impression on their children's development, though usually they don't.

We do know, however, that it is in the first few years of life that the personality patterns of the future adult are set – viz the quote from that famous Greek philosopher, Aristotle, who said something like 'give me the boy until the age of seven and I will give you a receipt'. By an amazing coincidence, when the government heard about the educational and developmental process that Aristotle offered to young people, they invented the Greek word for 'molesting' and gave him exactly seven years. Which only goes to show the value of a smart lawyer even in those days.

By another amazing coincidence, a friend of mine who isn't even Greek has just thrust an urgent note into my hand, suggesting that the famous Aristotle quote I was using back there was actually said on his behalf by someone else, more than likely this Spanish Jesuit chappie, St Ignatius of Mazola, I think it says, but neither of us can read the writing. Anyway, where was I?

What, then, are the characteristics of a good parent and good parenting? What is it that turns, say, a young girl or woman into a mother? Well, in a word – pregnancy. But yet, it's not quite as simple as that. Although on many occasions it *is* as simple as that if you're

not careful, which is why you should read the next section first. Preferably before you read this one.

Family Planning

Family planning is actually a difficult concept. By which I really mean that many family planning methods are quite difficult to grasp. Or rather that there are lots of different ways of planning a family, and an equal number of myths and misconceptions.

One of these is the idea that you can't become pregnant whilst breast-feeding. I don't mean just at that particular minute, I mean during what we fathers call 'lactation'. Well, actually many women *are* sub-fertile during lactation, though in modern times I would say that young children have a contraceptive effect by different mechanisms, e.g. by wandering in and asking for a glass of water at midnight.

Perhaps one can best consider family planning techniques under two main headings – the mechanical or 'barrier' methods, and the 'hormonal' methods.

Among the mechanical methods are the well-known prophylactics, which a German friend of mine used to call 'preservatives'. And you can see what he meant, although the shop assistant in Boots couldn't and sold him a tin of creosote.

The hormonal methods are far too well known to be detailed here, though of course one has to remember that Mother Nature (or, if successful, Non-Mother Nature) has invented her own hormonal contraceptive millions of years ago. It's called the headache.

Anyway, I will conclude this section by reminding you of one of the many misunderstandings surrounding this subject. It appears that ten years ago in a country far, far away (Camden Town) a man called Mr O'Shaughnessy had nineteen children. Since it was the year of the Queen's Award to Industry, he got a great honour in the Birthday List. Accordingly, the Equerry-in-Waiting went round to their place in Camden Town and told Mrs O'Shaughnessy that Her Majesty had given Mr O'Shaughnessy a knighthood for his productivity and she said you can give him what you like but he won't wear it.

Twins

Twins are nature's revenge for man's attempts at family planning. There are two kinds of twins, *identical* and *non-identical*, though they are easily confused and I once asked a patient if her twins were identical, to which she replied, 'Only the boy is.'

Which also reminds me of a nice Italian lady whom I looked after and when I asked her how many children she had she said she had three, one of each. Which turned out to be surprisingly accurate in her particular case, but that is another matter.

Anyway, twins can tell us an enormous amount about the role of inheritance, but I wouldn't let them if I were you. The main advantage of being a twin is that there is somebody close to you who really understands and listens to you, which is why I wanted to be a twin. My wish later came true and with the help of the Rotary Club I have now been twinned with the City of Nuremburg. As I understand it, this means that I have the complete freedom of the city, provided that I pay for their roadsweeping service.

More research is clearly needed in this matter.

Bodylanguageology

In surveying the function of spoken and written communication in the human species, insufficient attention is paid to those forms of communication that are neither spoken nor written, e.g. fighting and shouting. And, of course, body language. I shall therefore deal in some detail with human body language and gestures. Wisely is it said that one picture is worth a thousand words. Unfortunately we couldn't afford that kind of picture, so here are the words instead.

BODY LANGUAGE

Everybody knows about body language – it's what people say to each other by gestures etc when they're not actually talking or speaking e.g. during marriage. Studies on gregarious animals like buffalo, sticklebacks, kippers and so on, show that body language has evolved from a need to regularise certain functions of the herd e.g. mating, territorial occupation, vote rigging, etc. As the well-known animal behaviourist, Alan Hodkins, pointed out from his experiences in Michigan, it could be postulated that, in Man, body language has an inherent and innate biological value as a signal, which cannot be over-ridden by more recently-evolved rational processes, including thought and verbal language. This was an interesting argument, but the girl stuck to her story and Hodkins got two years. However, it does highlight a fascinating enigma of body language – how can we understand it and use it when we haven't been taught it, as opposed to say French, which Man cannot understand or use even when he has been taught it? Well, the answer is that body language actually evolved right along with our species and is as much a part of humankind as having a vestigial appendix, an opposable thumb and haemorrhoids. In other words, body language is something that goes on all the time in health, although there are certain pathological states in which the amount of ongoing body language is reduced or abolished, for instance in rigor mortis – although some post-Laingians believe that even that is making a statement about something or other, burial costs perhaps. Anyway, it's easiest to look at body language under the headings of the major emotional content of what it conveys (see *Yiddish*, next book).

SIGNALS CONVEYING AGGRESSION

Perhaps aggression is the prime example of the value of a species-specific biological signal. On the other hand, perhaps it isn't. I don't know. Anyway, the point is that there are lots of ways in which body language can convey aggression and most of us have no difficulty recognising them, when we're getting mugged, for instance. The signals originate from the physiological actions of the hormones that cause aggression (adrenalin, nor-adrenalin and nor-nor-east-adrenalin). These hormones cause the pupils to dilate, the lips to snarl and the shoulders to hunch, allowing our ape ancestors a survival advantage over weaker foes e.g. in the crush at the January sales. As time passed, these signals became ritualised into symbols of aggression, allowing the animal to appear to be aggressive without going to the bother of making up the adrenalin fresh. Thus to quote the illustrious zoologist Claude Klumpkopff, when a tiger is snarling, he is actually saying 'This is what I could look like if I got angry', and it is a preamble, not a threat. Mind you, they buried Klumpkopff in eleven separate places in Borneo, so perhaps it doesn't mean the same with all tigers. Anyway, we humans do similar things. Thus we raise our shoulders, curl back our lips and narrow our eyes (all biological signals which mean 'Beware foe, my name is Robin Day'). These nonspoken signals are so powerful that opponents will react with fear and alarm, even when they accompany verbal language (e.g. words) that seems friendly, like our Prime Minister before she had The Lessons – and after. Some people want to know whether any of this can be useful in daily life. Well, the answer is yes, a bit – you should take as much care over your non-verbal communication as over your language, and if your body language gives you away, you can enhance your career-prospects by learning to conceal it, e.g. living in a tent, or something like that. Or just stop worrying about expressing aggression and get a job with National Car Parks.

SEXUAL SIGNALS

Body language is pretty important when it comes to expressing sexual attractions, too. After all, when you think about it, the survival of the species depends even more heavily on sex than it does on aggression, unless you support Millwall. It is precisely *because* sex is so necessary (no matter what your wife says) that the expression of attraction by body language is so easy to initiate (and so difficult to pretend not to be happening if you're trying to play hard to get). However, even in communities as lowly as that of the common frog, complex courtship patterns go on, with the male frogs demonstrating sexual interest by a peculiar discoloration at the base of the thumb (which is pretty obvious to the ladies, and that's all that counts). Thus, during the season, dominant males will mate with many females, while non-dominant 'loser' males end up emptying the ashtrays and making coffee downstairs, even though everyone respects them really because they've got nice personalities. Repeated on a cosmic scale, this is why all species, as they have evolved, have become nastier and nastier. Human sexual body language is based on similar mechanisms – the blush, for instance, is a vestige of the oestral signal of the female baboons (who blush easily anyway, particularly the Presbyterians). Similarly, the closing of one eye (the 'wink'), the pursing of the lips (the 'pout') and the flicking of the tongue over the lower lip are all based on things that other animals do, particularly cobras. It is a curious fact that, as we have become more civilised and clothed, sexual body language (and bodies) have become more ambiguous and liable to misinterpretation. My advice is that, unless you think you're Desmond Morris, ask first – better still, get it in writing.

THE DOCTOR ANSWERS YOUR QUESTIONS

Q: Sometimes I get a feeling that there is an animal consciousness or spirit within me, endowed with its own intelligence and natural power. Could this be true?

A: Yes. It might be a tapeworm.

THE V-SIGN

The most amazing thing about the V-sign is that not only is it an instant indication of virulent antipathy, but also Man is the only animal that can get it right. For many animal species any attempt is fraught with difficulty, e.g. pigs have the correctly shaped hands but can't bend their elbows; ants haven't got the proper number of fingers; and octopuses haven't got a snowball's chance in a frying-pan – and don't hate anyone enough anyway.

Medically speaking (or rather, gesturing), the traditional British V-sign comprises presentation of the extensor surfaces of index and middle fingers, raised from the meridian position to eye-level by a sharp flexion of the elbow, signifying to the recipient that his wife and that Other Gentleman are more than good friends. Of course, its adulterous origin is now lost in the mists of antiquity (as is most adultery, if you're really careful), so that the gesture now merely signals the signaller's desire that the signallee be fruitful and multiply elsewhere.

It is interesting to note that the Italians don't use the index and middle fingers for a V-sign (I'm not sure they use them for anything come to that, but this is a time for goodwill to all men and I suppose that includes foreigners as well). What the Italians do is to use the index and little fingers, folding the middle two down under the thumb. This is known as the 'cornuto' after the horns of the deer, though whether it's because deer-hunters are good at being co-respondents or because deer are notoriously unfaithful, I don't know. The Americans by contrast, simply present the middle finger – not surprising really, the Americans have to abbreviate everything, don't they? Though, to be fair, the American single-finger gesture has less to do with your wife than with your toilet arrangements (which is also true of a lot of marriages – and divorces come to that).

WINKING

Winking just happens to be the ancient name for the second largest city in Northern China, which is where the method of briefly closing one eye while keeping the other open was first invented and perfected, at a time when we in the West were still barbarians and savages living in primaeval conditions, i.e. 1928.

What does a wink mean? The answer is that a wink generally signifies communication at a higher level than that of the overt subject matter. It can be a disclaimer, signifying to an observer that the content of the conversation is false, e.g. a wink accompanying an apparently factual statement such as 'one previous owner', 'my wife doesn't understand me', 'I'll always respect you' etc. In this context, the wink is acting as a disclaimer like those things at the bottom of estate agents' and theatrical agents' letters that say 'nothing in this letter constitutes a contract' (though, in my opinion, it would be more accurate to say, 'nothing in this letter constitutes a fact', or even 'nothing in this letter constitutes anything at all').

That is the general or non-specific semiological value of the wink – but it also has specific or contextual value. In certain cultures a wink can signal the availability of sexual favour in circumstances where direct communication of that idea would be ill-advised – this includes board meetings, out-of-town conferences, the Appeal Court, Royal garden parties, etc.

As a come-on signal, in the 'business community', the wink is clearly understood by all those who sell their personal services for mere gain, e.g. ladies of the night, journalists, private doctors and allied trades. Even so, it's best to get it in writing first.

THE RASPBERRY

Even at a technical level, the raspberry is a fascinating phenomenon. Phonetic experts have defined the raspberry as a noise made by extrusion of the tongue between lightly compressed lips with initiation of bilateral contraction of the buccinator (or cheek) muscles causing intermittent expulsion of air in a phonetic distribution known as the interrupted plosive or farting noise. It is, of course, an example of onomatopoeia (well, sort of) and is correctly spelt PBFLLT in its shortened ('dry') form or FHTHWOOPHSSHFFT in the fuller ('wet') form for people with false teeth.

But what does it signify? Oh, come on, you know very well what it signifies. It signifies that the donor thinks the recipient is no more than a load of retro-expelled hot air, as Shakespeare would have put it 'full of sound, and furry, and signifying nothing'.

What is really nice about blowing a raspberry at some pompous oaf or other is that you can put some real effort into it. A V-sign or shouting 'bum' are all right in their way, but you don't expend energy and feel, somehow, unfulfilled. After a proper, deeply-inhaled, full-tongued, five-litre, Force Nine raspberry you're knackered for a good ten minutes. Your spleen is properly vented, honour is satisfied and there is a psychogenic ventilation of cosmic proportions. And universal intelligibility. A raspberry transcends national frontiers and boundaries. It means the same to Hispanic, Roman and Celt; it unites all mankind in a common bond of contempt for our fellow beings. And at this special time surely that, at least, is something for which to be grateful. And if you don't agree, then PBFLLT to you.

THE DOCTOR ANSWERS YOUR QUESTIONS

Q: Hello, I'm from the Conservative Party and I'm just interested in assessing our market penetration among the professional classes. I wonder if you could tell me your impression, as a doctor and articulate communicator, of the policies of the Government as put before Parliament at the opening?

A: FHTHWOOPHSSHFFT.

Q: I see – is that spelt with four F's, or three F's and a PH?

Movementology

Among all the animal species, Man is by far the most mobile in terms of the earth's surface (with certain notable exceptions, e.g. the M6). Even so, Man's exceptional mobility is due, fundamentally, to his skeletal system, his upright posture and his desire to get out of the house. Here are a few facts about each of them.

THE HAZARDS OF ERECT POSTURE

Man is a biped. (It's a funny word that – I always used to think it was pronounced as if it rhymed with 'piped' and that it meant man was a creature designed for biping and who would bipe whenever he could.) Yes, man is a biped which means that he walks on two legs which are known in biophysical jargon as the left leg and the right leg, but not necessarily in that order.

As a biped, Man has a great deal in common with the ostrich, the penguin, the kangaroo and any daddy-long-legs that happen to have lost four of their legs. But what distinguishes Man from most other bipeds, including whales, motorcycles, toasting forks etc, is his famous Erect Posture. I can't quite recall all the details, but I remember the key words Man, Erect Posture, The Opposable Thumb and Bipedal Gait from the same section of my O-level biology notes. I think maybe Man first tried walking upright on his Opposable Thumbs but then gave up and had a crack at Bipedality, then did all the other primate stuff, *viz* giving birth to live young, symbolic language, insider trading, vandalising phone-boxes etc.

Anyway, the evolution thingy doesn't matter – standing upright began thousands and thousands of years ago and is clearly here to stay even among people who voted for the Alliance. Which I did. (Clearly the evolution of the Opposable Thumb hasn't progressed to the Opposable Government yet, ahahaha, no, just kidding, good for Britain, good for Britain, well done, well done, jolly good show – oh bum, bang goes my knighthood, never mind, didn't really want it anyway.)

Yes, so man adopted erect posture in order to free up his opposable thumbs from the business of being walked on, but little did he realise that erect posture carried certain hazards, known in the American language as the downside (thus 'standing upright has its downside' etc etc). And these hazards of erect posture can be loosely divided into two categories, or tightly into three categories, depending, the VAT's the same either way. Loosely, then, they can be divided into the mechanical and the visceral downside of keeping the backside upside.

The Mechanical Sequelae of Bipedality

There can be no doubt that man's adopting an erect posture has been the cause of many of his subsequent medical afflictions. I should imagine that quadruped pre-anthropoid apes viewed the early bipedal variant species with much distrust, and when the two-legged ones developed low back pain, varicose veins and haemorrhoids I bet all the quadrupeds said told you no good would come of it, if God had intended us to stand upright he would have built the sky taller, stamp out bidpedality, mandatory testing for anyone who looks half like a biped, don't let them near my children etc etc.

Anyway, once man stood up and looked around at the wild, fecund and unspoiled world that he could, and soon would, dominate, man immediately realised – in a moment of profound insight – that he had a nasty pain in the small of his back. For it is a medical fact that the small of his back, a.k.a. the lumbar lordosis, is designed to give spring and bounce to a fast-moving galloping quadruped and would have been a great invention if man had decided to evolve into a racehorse. Though I can't imagine who we would have had as jockeys, maybe chimpanzees with perhaps alligators as bookmakers – which is certainly the way it looked at Aintree this year as far as I was concerned.

As things turned out, we decided not to evolve into racehorses or tigers or anything, but we evolved into man and our lumbar lordosis evolved into fibrositis and an excuse for not papering the spare room etc.

So it can be seen that we owe our backache to our primaeval and atavistic desire to oppose our thumbs – but our backs are not the only things that suffer. Our hips are similar. Well, mine are anyway (although the left is more similar than the right ahaha). The hip joints of ordinary quadruped mammals are designed to support the weight of the back part of the body only, namely the hypochondria, haunches, flanks, shanks, hanks and bum. The hips are not designed to support the weight of the shoulders and head – well, not your own anyway (though I could lay my weary head and shoulders on the hips of Cybil Sheppard any day).

But, of course, with upright posture there isn't anything to support the top half of the body because it's right on top of the bottom half, thus doubling the weight on the hip joints and all stations south. Now, of course, you may say, 'But surely the hip joints of an elephant support a total of two and a half tons (two and a quarter, if they're on a diet), and they don't get arthritis.' But, haha, that shows how much you know because (a) elephants don't stand on their hind legs and run up stairs and stand in queues at the post office for hours and break dance and (b) if they did, they'd get arthritis (and the post office queues would be longer, though that's difficult to believe) and (c) if we had the hip joints of an elephant we wouldn't get arthritis or (d) jeans to fit us either.

It is therefore clear that we have selected for ourselves a mode of locomotion fraught with biomechanical hazard (and you're speaking to a man who once tried to do the Mashed Potato, so I know of what I speak) – but yet more hazards are produced by the effect on the soft tissues inside the body which, subject to a change in gravity, develop a tendency to protrude out and see what the fuss is all about.

THE DOCTOR IS INVENTIVE

Q: Hi, I'm a chiropractor. And, well, I've just invented a chiropractic miracle – it's a sort of extendable lumbar brace that fits into your lumbar lordosis and when you get back pain you crank it open a bit and it lifts up your spine and relieves the pain. The trouble is I can't think what to call it – have you got any ideas?

A: How about 'The LumbarJack'?

WALKING

Although you might think that it's the easiest thing in the world, the apparently simple act of walking is actually immensely complex and difficult, particularly in Detroit where you can be arrested for not owning a car. Now, when it comes to the mechanism of walking, neuro-physiologists in Alberta have spent years studying the pathways of nerves in the brain and spinal cord and have concluded that successful walking depends on two critical factors. They're called legs. No, that's not right, they're called the neural mechanisms of balance and power (not 'balance of power', by the way, which has nothing to do with any form of movement or forward progress or anything else). The point is that you need a whole bunch of muscles to stand up and move your leg. Thus the quadriceps muscle flexes the hip (forward) and lifts the leg up, the hamstrings extend the leg (backwards) at the hip, the sartorius muscle twists it round but no-one knows exactly what is required to unfailingly get the leg over. Or they never told me anyway. Now the really difficult part of walking is that as you bring one set of muscles into action, you have to relax the other set. It's like those quaint wooden figures that swing in and out of little wooden doors whenever the weather changes (our political system is based on the same principle by the way, but it's a bit slower and less sensitive to the climate). Anyway, the part of the body in charge of co-ordinating this task is the cerebellum and it receives messages from the legs (or, in the case of Americans, from their lawyers) and matches this with information received from the organs of balance which are situated in each ear (except for journalists who have none at all). Acting on information received, the cerebellum then allows one set of muscles to relax and the leg to move. If the cerebellum has been misinformed or misled (and it's a pretty gullible and wanton organ at the best of times), then it may give the instruction to relax all sets of locomotor muscles at once, in which case you fall down. Usually, the cerebellum realises its mistake and complies with the next set of instructions often to do with giving your wife the car keys. Actually, compared with the complexities of walking, driving a car seems an absolute doddle, so perhaps it's no surprise that people think they can drive when they can't manage to walk.

JOGGING

When you come to think about it, jogging is really like designer-walking. What it really does is affect many different body systems in

a fairly general way – thus it affects the pulse rate and puts that up, it causes a rise in blood flow to skin and muscle, affects the respiration rate and bosom movement causing both to rise (hence the phrase 'upwardly mobile'). Now, American jogging has had some dreadfully bad press recently because of some people suffering from a rather rare syndrome called dropping dead. Health experts in the States (which means absolutely everybody) have two responses to this problem. Firstly, they claim that the people might just as easily have dropped dead earlier, or been struck by lightning, or become president, or something just as bad, if they hadn't happened to be jogging. And secondly, that dropping dead needn't necessarily be perceived as a totally negative health experience. Particularly if you're insured. In Italy, sudden death is regarded as one of the few things that make jogging a spectator sport, whereas in Britain we regard it as something done by the hooligan fringe which the average law-abiding jogger wouldn't be seen dead doing. There is, however, no doubt that jogging on the whole is an immensely beneficial form of locomotion and promotes health-modifying interactions with many other forms of locomotion, e.g. lorries.

DANCING

Physiologically speaking, dancing is even more complex than either walking or jogging although it usually pays better. What ordinary people don't realise when watching ballet is that when a ballet dancer is standing still on tip-toe a vast amount of energy is being consumed every second merely to keep absolutely still. Mind you, they said exactly the same about the budget of Covent Garden and the Arts Council fell for it hook, line and sinker, so maybe we should try saying the same thing about the NHS. Anyway, the point is that they consume a tremendous amount of energy and it has been calculated that an average ballet corps doing *Swan Lake* uses enough energy to give a week's supply of light to a city the size of Huddersfield, excluding the theatre, which is a bit of a shame since no-one would go to see the ballet in the dark – not that they do anyway, the silly philistines.

In Russia on the other hand, ballet is regarded as a national sport like athletics and seeking asylum, and the ballet dancers train for it by taking anabolic steroids and blood doping and learning how to fake their chromosome tests. Perhaps that shows that the Russians have a greater faith in physiology than us, or perhaps it shows that we just have lots of fun dressing up in super frocks. No, that was unfair, I didn't mean it.

OTHER MEANS OF LOCOMOTION

As the process of evolution proceeded, many different means of locomotion were tried out by various species. Thus the fin, the flipper, the wing, the hoof, and the tail have all been adapted, each in their own unique way, to help animals speed through water, land and air. However, some have been less successful than others and have died out. Perhaps the most extraordinary discovery of all came from some fossils of dinosaurs found in the Le Brea tar pits in California where the bones of a previously unknown reptile were found. It apparently had a low, flat body with a hard skeleton outside, with four very short legs each ending in a small wheel. Palaeontologists believe that this was nature's attempt to design a skateboard and it became extinct in less than three years. Which is exactly what happened in 1979, so it just shows that we never learn, do we?

Addictionology

ALCOHOL

As a well-known doctor and broadcaster with a major interest in alcohol addiction and its effects on human physiology, one of the most common questions I am asked is, 'What will you have, doctor?' Well, like most responsible members of society I have a strict rule

about drinking while on duty – I never do it unless someone else is paying. Alcohol has a lot of different effects on the body and the mind – and sometimes both. As a medical student, I spent a considerable amount of effort researching this field using a control population of young adults, usually nurses aged 23. I thought you might like the benefit of our findings, though the names and telephone numbers have been changed to protect the guilty. As usual I shall remain anonymous.

The Chemistry of Alcohol

Chemically speaking, what we call 'alcohol' is a relatively simple compound known correctly as ethyl alcohol or ethanol. This comparatively small molecule is one of a family of larger, complex sister compounds which have different first names, such as methyl alcohol, and the less famous ones like propyl alcohol, butyl alcohol, futile alcohol and puerile alcohol (found in immature wines like Beaujolais Nouveau). Apart from these sisters, there are the parent compounds which are known colloquially as wood alcohol (or 'Woody') and Mrs Wood Alcohol together with the maiden aunt Bloody Mary, the disreputable French cousin Absinthe, the Mexican black sheep of the family, Tequila Sunrise, and the sweet old granny, Sanatogen.

Now, what these compounds have in common is the chemical structure which includes a hydroxyl group on the terminal carbon atom (written as –OH, or HO– in the laevo isomer). That is why chemists are constantly trying to produce complex polyvalent alcohols that can be written as C_{24}–H_{60}–HO–HO–HO, which would be a real hit at the lab Christmas party, if nowhere else. Anyway, it is the terminal hydroxyl group that gives the alcohols their particular affinity for more complex and larger chemical structures, e.g. Coke, soda, olives etc. This is also what makes you drunk (*see below, particularly before you fall down*), though not what gives you the hangover (it's probably the peanuts that do that).

However, the metabolism of alcohol inside the body is not simple – nor painless. Once the alcohol molecules get inside the body (albeit briefly, e.g. beer), they move about rapidly in the bloodstream, interacting with erythrocytes, desaturating phosphate buffers, meeting new friends, laughing loudly, and dropping ash on the carpet. They then migrate to the brain (usually before the police arrive) where they produce a series of effects so far-reaching and complex that I shall leave them to the next paragraph.

There will now be a short pause for refreshment. If you wish to have a drink in the interval between paragraphs, please remember to order it before the start. Thank you.

Alcohol and the Brain

Now let me ask you the following question: would you believe that alcohol is actually a depressant (apart from when you have to pay for it yourself)? Sorry, time's up, and the answer is NO, i.e. no, you wouldn't believe it. Well, it just shows how wrong you can be, because it is – alcohol is actually a potent inhibitor of brain functions (try having lunch with a journalist if you don't believe me).

However what is so extraordinary is that the parts of the brain most susceptible to this inhibition are the inhibitory pathways themselves. In physiological terms, what happens is that the major bio-parametric negative-feedback inhibitory systems become down-regulated by sub-maximal loops resulting in a high-excitational state with minimal signal–noise ratio, known to neurophysiologists as 'getting pissed'.

What happens after that depends on where you are and who you're with. But either way, perhaps the most important question is: if the alcohol molecules move around the brain for such a short time, how come they leave it in such a mess the next morning? Anybody? Thank you, Tebbit, but Currie's hand was up first. Yes, alcohol is a major diuretic (please *stop* giggling, if we can't be adult about things like bladders and kidneys, I'll sit down right now and let Edwina tell the class what's wrong with society. There now, that's better).

Thus alcohol is a diuretic and causes temporary dehydration, aided and abetted by the salt peanuts, Brie, pork scratchings and, in my opinion, loud music, which certainly seems to scare something out of people over the age of 21. Prolonged exposure to alcohol affects the brain very seriously, producing various encephalopathies and Korsakoff's syndrome in which short-term memory is lost and the patient confabulates, which means making up stories to cover up the gaps. Unfortunately, I can't remember anything about Korsakoff's syndrome even though I looked it up this morning, so I just made all this stuff up as I went along.

Alcohol and the Liver

Everyone knows that alcohol can produce permanent changes in the liver, e.g. liver in white-wine sauce with chopped shallots and mushrooms. So, if you have a liver scan and it shows that the mushrooms have appeared, you may safely assume you're in danger. However, before that stage, liver damage can be very subtle and unnoticeable (particularly if you've got a good tailor).

The interesting thing is that, to a large extent, the susceptibility to alcohol-damage is inherited – so that if you wish to drink moderately and survive you ought to choose your parents with great care. Perhaps this could be the new target of the Unborn Child's Right To Choice movement – offering the foetus a fair chance to have a look round its parents' hepatic function and wine cellars before deciding whether to be born or not. It would certainly save some disappointment later.

TRANQUILLISERS

Say what you will about alcohol, including 'cheers' etc, it is only *one* of society's drugs of addiction. Some of these society has deemed as 'acceptable' which is why it's so nice to go to society's parties, etc. There is, however, an untold story – that of tranquillisers, their origins and their use in society. I take this opportunity to untell the untellable.

Tranquillisers – Their History

It is not generally known that one of the world's best known tranquillisers was discovered by accident at the turn of the century by a young Swiss cuckoo-clock thief. His name was Hoffman La Roche, which in Franco-German means 'Headman The Rock' (apparently he was into heavy metal music – of which there was very little in Zürich in 1902).

Anyway, he was on the run from the police of the elite Clock Squad and, panicky and upset, he fell to the ground and threw a full temper-tantrum, known in the complex technical jargon of transactional psychotherapy as a 'paddy'.

In those antediluvian days of psychiatry, such behaviour would probably have been treated by the so-called *Schmoltz-Endelbaum Regime,* which consisted mostly of sending the patient straight to bed and no watching television (which was also fairly easy to arrange in 1902).

It therefore seemed that young Hoffman had much to fear, and he bit the ground in his frenzy. In the process, he swallowed some of the peculiar, yellowish soil for which the neighbourhood was renowned and, to his amazement, he immediately felt calm and tranquil.

The rest is history. That soil contained approximately 92 per cent diazepam mingled with aluminium oxides, silicates and a modicum of dogs' doings. Hoffman realised the therapeutic value of the soil immediately and it is now the site of the world's largest and richest Valium mine. Some 100,000 tons of the drug are brought to the surface every day by teams of sweating miners, who are rewarded heavily if they find a vein rich in the larger size tablets.

And to this day, the city of Zürich revels in the success founded by its most famous son, and basks in its reputation as a source of the world's most vital minerals (the name Zürich actually means 'too rich' which indeed most inhabitants are).

Actually I now realise that I have been copying this from the wrong page of my *Boy's Own History of the Universe & Meccano*. I think that was how truffles were first discovered. Or maybe krugerrands. Or maybe food poisoning.

Anyway, I apologise, so let's move on.

Tranquillisers – Their Chemistry

Most of the common tranquillisers are *benzodiazepines*, a large family of chemical molecules that comprise the original Valium, sister molecules Librium and Fannium, the twins Jimmium and Johnium, the mad uncle Maxium and his midget wife, Minimum, plus a whole tribe of camp-followers such as Frisium, Floppium, Sillium, Geranium, Millium, Billium, etc, which all have amine-substituted ethyl-rich side chains, acne and bad breath.

Most pharmacologists are familiar with the mechanism of action of these interesting and versatile molecules. I, on the other hand, am not. However, certain general comments about the mode of action can be made. For instance, absorption of the drug from the gastro-intestinal tract into the systemic circulation is essential. Which means the drugs don't work until you take them out of the bottle and swallow them. Although certain persons – sensitive to the so-called 'placebo effect' of psychological reassurance – claim to feel better just holding the bottle.

Interestingly, though, in a controlled, clinical comparison using 35 blindfolded neurotics, none could tell the difference in relaxation produced by identically-shaped bottles containing Librium, Ovaltine, two pages of a book by Jeffrey Archer, or a corner of their old cot-blanket. (As it happens, I am a strong placebo-responder myself, which is why I always prepare for sleep by taking two tablets containing 5mg of cot-blanket. However, that is my problem, not yours.)

Tranquillisers – Their Home Phone Numbers

There has been much controversy concerning the major site of action of tranquillisers in the human. Personally speaking, I always thought they acted pretty powerfully on the human downbelows and would take them whenever I didn't fancy a cold shower. Which was always. But, in fact, it is now known that they work on the human brain (which is why they never work when estate agents take them). Sorry.

Anyway, benzodiazepines decrease cortical hyperactivity, raise the threshold of pyramidal cells to focal discharge, inhibit the chemotactic trigger zone, reduce the federal deficit and encourage alpha rhythms, reflation, limbic system downregulation and REM sleep – if it's a bull market, anyway.

Another theory suggests that the main site of action for the tranquillisers is Switzerland. This may be true, because while the

rest of the world has been tearing its eyes out in a frenzy of hysterical panic buying, panic selling and panic panicking, the Swiss haven't turned a hair.

Either they're all on tranquillisers or they've all got shares in them.

Or both.

Poisonology

As the nation's leading authority on self-medication and health problems around the home, I am frequently consulted by desperate patients with allergy problems who urgently need to get rid of musty, smelly objects around the house – usually spouses or aunts. Many of these consultations contain a request for a list of potent vegetable poisons or toxins, while others request more advanced advice such as the number of a good lawyer. Naturally, the Hippocratic Oath and the ethics of my profession prevent me from transmitting information that might be used to shorten other people's lives, unless there are exceptional circumstances such as increasing the sales of this book. Here is that information.

(H.M. Government Health Warning: The World's Most Lethal Poisons May Damage Your Health – Wear Gloves While Pouring)

BOTULISM

Botulism is the disease caused by swallowing some of the poison produced by the bacterium **Clostridium botulinus**.

It is the most lethal substance known on earth – a thousand molecules can kill a man, or maybe one molecule can kill a thousand men, I forget. Either way, *Clostridium botulinus* is incredibly poisonous and nasty and was named after Marcus Botulinus, the Roman book critic (and not, as is commonly supposed, named after the contemporary scientist Botulinus Pauling, although he can make you pretty ill, too).

Now, you may be wondering how you get botulism or, more importantly, how you give it. Well, it doesn't come free with four gallons or more, that's for certain: it's actually a bacterium that lives in the earth, though I can't quite remember how it gets there. I seem to remember that doggy do's have something to do with it – which is true of most of the problems of the world. Anyway, the thing about your wily clostridium bug is that when the going gets rough, he rolls up into a ball and tucks his head in, forming something called a **spore**. As such he becomes damnably difficult to trek and kill because you can't see the whites of his eyes to shoot at, even if he had any, which he doesn't, and even if you could shoot at them, which you can't.

Now, none of this is a problem unless you preserve food in cans at home. The thing about home-canning is, fortunately, most of us can't (ahaha). But those that can can, do. And occasionally, clostridium spores sneak in with the preserved food (e.g. particularly fruit – which can be a food, despite what British Rail buffets would have you believe) and they hide in there when the food is bottled, canned and pickled. And if you're a home-canner you might not heat it just enough to kill the spores, which unroll and wake up to find themselves in the midst of, say, a can of apple sauce, surrounded by food, peace, tranquillity and joy unbounded (assuming they're not bright enough to realise that they're in Iowa, let's say, which would certain ruin it for me).

So the clostridia wake up, eat, and procreate (an enviable existence, come to think of it) and repay the generosity of their landlords by manufacturing toxic wastes, and starting off an Iowa apple botulism outbreak. I think there's a moral in there about the true meaning of being as American as apple pie, but I'm damned if I can think of it.

BELLADONNA

Belladonna was the poison most popular with the Borgias (Lucrezia, Vincenzo, Lorenzo and Zeppo). It means 'beautiful woman' but I can't remember why, unless maybe the Borgias believed that the only beautiful woman is a dead woman – a view certainly not espoused by the extant descendant of their ill-starred line, the wonderfully entertaining Victor Borgia, who I'm sure wouldn't poison anybody, least of all a beautiful woman.

Anyway, *belladonna*, like all the others, is also the most lethal substance known on earth, though I once had some Japanese sake that must have been a close second – they called it 'rocket fuel' because if you break wind after drinking it you tend to land at Edwards Air Force Base.

You get belladonna from a plant known as the 'deadly nightshade'. Tinctures of belladonna were used in Victorian hospitals and were dished out by a designated nurse who became known as the 'deadly nightnurse' to distinguish her from the more senior nursing sisters who were called the 'venus flytrap', though I may be getting a little confused.

More research is clearly needed here.

THE FLY AGARIC

The *fly agaric* is an incredibly poisonous mushroom known among its close circle of friends (all of whom are deceased) as **Amanita phalloides**.

It is named *phalloides* because its shape resembles what zoologists call in technical jargon a *thingy* (as seen on a male horse and I don't mean the bridle) and it was given the first name *Amanita* to remind the unwary of the danger of fooling about with Portuguese au pairs.

It lives on the forest floor where it merges unobtrusively with other less lethal mushrooms, blending in with the ground cover, nibbling canapés, nodding and smiling, speaking only when it's spoken to and leaving the bathroom as tidy as it found it.

Once swallowed, however, it is a mushroom of a different colour altogether. Like *botulinus* toxin,it is also the most lethal substance known on earth, and produces effects that are known in pharmacology as *anticholinergic*, which are sometimes useful, but in excess bring certain hazards, e.g. stopping your heart.

The main trouble with your fly agaric is, like policemen and taxis, there's never one around when you want one.

PTOMAINE POISONING

Ptomaine poisoning is a form of acute food poisoning usually reported in America and named after the place where it was discovered, i.e. the Ptomac River, or maybe named after the famous Indian Chief Ptomaine a.k.a. Little Running Belly.

Either way it had nothing whatever to do with the French flatulologist, Le Ptomaine. Ptomaines are actually a group of substances found in decomposing material – particularly meat and poultry that is a bit 'gamy', e.g. ptarmigan, ptartridge etc, and well-rotted vegetation, such as ptomato, ptotato etc.

Unfortunately, I seem to have forgotten everything I was ever taught about ptomaine poisoning, apart from the fact that it's incredibly unpleasant. Or perhaps it isn't, I forget. Let's move on.

THE DOCTOR SAYS IT WITH FLOWERS

Q: Are there any other flowers which are really dangerous?

A: Well, a friend of mine robbed a bank using just a bunch of flowers as an offensive weapon. He got two years because they called it robbery with violets.

ARSENIC

Despite what you think, arsenic is actually a chemical element, which means that if you break it down into its constituent parts you find that they consist of the same stuff. I believe the same is true of many other chemical elements, e.g. caviar, tapioca, the Reform Club etc. Anyway, arsenic is actually a *metal*, rather like silver, though nobody ever bothered to make cutlery out of it ('if you want me, I'll be downstairs polishing the family arsenic'). However, it is chiefly important for the chemical salts it can make.

There are two common ones used as pesticides – *Paris green*, which is really *copper acetoarsenate*, and *Fowler's solution*, which is *potassium arsenite* and was discovered by the gentleman-chemist Jasper Fowler, whose maxim 'one arsenite is enough for . . .' NONONONONO. Sorry. And I was doing so well.

Now, there are two quite extraordinary things about arsenic, but, sadly, I've forgotten both of them. However, I have remembered that it lurks in your skin and *adnexae* long after you've snuffed it – hence the forensic use of measuring arsenic in the body's hair and nails. Apparently, some boffins exhumed dear dead Napoleon and found his hair was absolutely loaded with arsenic, and concluded that he'd been poisoned to death, though my theory was that his hair was so brittle with arsenic that he couldn't do a thing with it and died of shame.

THALLIUM

Thallium has been known for decades as a toxic poison and is not, as I once thought, derived from a rude-looking toadstool shaped a bit like a thallic symbol. No, thallium is a common constituent of many commercial depilatories, although by a fortunate coincidence I have forgotten what depilatories are. Unless they're something the clergy wear, or maybe they're suppositories for the ears. No, they're not, they're stuff for removing unwanted excess hair (from the Latin words 'de-' meaning off or from, 'pila-' meaning hairs and '-tories' meaning unwanted excess conservatives).

Anyway, Agatha Christie knew all about thallium and knew precisely which depilatories it could be found in, and which ones were harmless – or maybe she didn't and shaved her legs to be on the safe side. Either way, I do know for a fact that when it came to unwanted facial hair, Agatha had a secret supply of *arrggghhhh*. Tee hee, just fooling. (*Note to readers who take things literally: this was a joke. When looking for a facial depilatory do not use arrggghhh, or any product containing it.*)

SPANISH FLY

I must confess that I'm a little uncertain about Spanish fly – I seem to remember that it isn't actually a fly at all but a rather pathetic kind of beetle, and it isn't Spanish, although it has got bedroom eyes (1,800 of them) and oily back legs.

Anyway, the thing about Spanish fly is that it has this reputation as an aphrodisiac – which, medically speaking, is partly true. It is a known fact that ten milligrams of powdered male Spanish fly is immensely attractive to females, but, unfortunately, only to female Spanish flies. The main constituent is stuff called **cantharides** (which, until this morning, I thought were a group of islands half way between the Canaries and the Hebrides).

Now, *cantharides* is (or maybe are) basically an irritant – it causes nausea, vomiting and diarrhoea (mind you, so can the Canaries but that depends on your hotel) and causes even greater irritation to your bowel, rectum and the inside bits of your downbelows. I must admit I've never quite worked out how this makes a good aphrodisiac. Perhaps some women are attracted by vomiting and irritation – which certainly seems to be true in Australia.

CYANIDE

Unlike the other heavy-metal toxins, cyanide is neither a metal nor heavy. It is a salt-forming chemical group comprised of carbon and nitrogen, and is thus related chemically to other *-ide* compounds recognised in the laboratory, such as nitride, chloride, fluoride, fouride, bosside, crosside, teeside and seaside.

However, cyanide is the most poisonous of all and was known to the Romans, who used it to simplify debates in the Senate. As everybody knows, cyanide is found in bitter almonds, though I've never worked out how you can tell whether almonds are bitter or not, unless you taste them. This might be a bit of a problem since cyanide causes death in about a minute – which hardly gives you the chance to say, 'Gosh, these almonds are bitter, I'd much rather have a pickled walnut if you don't mind.'

Not many people know this, but cyanide is also found in cassava roots, the jet berry bush and hydrangeas – which means you should be very suspicious of anyone who takes away the bitter almonds when you complain and offers you a hydrangea instead. And this is the basis of every mother's advice to her children never to take sweets from hydrangeas. Actually, cyanide is mainly so poisonous because it clings to extremely important molecules inside your body and stops every single cell in your body from using oxygen, thus causing the metabolic equivalent of drowning on dry land. Seen from the point of view of cellular oxidative phosphorylation, this is a major setback and seen from the owner's point of view, it will certainly ruin your day.

THE DOCTOR CONTEMPLATES ETERNAL MYSTERIES

Q: I know this isn't your subject, but I was just reading this book on Tibet where the monks pick the successor to the Dalai Lama by finding a baby that's supposed to be the reincarnation of the deceased Dalai Lama. But what happens if they make a mistake and pick the wrong baby?

A: Steeped as I am in the mysteries of the Orient, I happen to know that this is what the Tibetan monks call the Falsa Lama.

Loonyology

We live in a peculiar age. Or at least, I do. Despite the burgeoning growth of science and the mechanistic understanding of the physical universe, there has been a popular movement towards mysticism and other 'crank' cults. Naturally, my attitude to these minority beliefs is that of the true and caring physician, i.e. I couldn't care less. Here are the most important facts on the current fads – alternative medicine, extra-sensory perception and astrology.

ALTERNATIVE MEDICINE

The role of alternative medicine in the health care of this nation is a controversial issue. According to some people anyway. As a medical writer, broadcaster and surrogate mother, I have never lacked the courage to boldly address the controversial issues that have been boldly addressed before. Particularly by me. It therefore behooves me to speak out at last on this sensitive and delicate issue. I have no alternative.

Why Alternative Medicine?

Currently, a lot of people believe that while modern doctors have improved their skills and prowess in treating diseases, they have lost their ability to care and to relate to their patients as human beings.

Now obviously this criticism does not apply to me, because, as a caring and humane medical practitioner, I recognise the merit in this viewpoint and I fully empathise with the motivations behind it – even though the published evidence suggests that alternative medicine is a load of horse-crap, packaged by a crew of sycophantic, glib cowboys who could sell ice to the Eskimos, particularly if they could call it holistic ice.

No no no, I didn't mean that, just kidding, ahahahaha.

Anyway, the people who are most attracted to alternative medicine are usually people who suffer from troublesome, but not life-threatening, conditions, e.g. living in Islington. No, that's not true either. Sorry.

Now lots of perfectly nice people have a recurring medical condition for which conventional medicine cannot offer a cure or do anything about, e.g. low back-ache, compulsive nose-picking, working in advertising, not wanting an independent deterrent etc. So the idea is that you go to an alternative medical practitioner, who cannot offer a cure or do anything about it either, but says so in a nice way and takes longer about it. Seriously, though, what alternative medical practitioners are good at is treating their patients as human beings in the context of their community and all its complex interrelationships.

Of course, a few conventional doctors are pretty nifty at that sort of approach, too, e.g. in California, although on this side of the Atlantic we call it something different, e.g. wife-swapping. However, the main point is absolutely undeniable – which is that we conventional doctors, as a group, are not all that good at certain high-tech complex medical doctor–patient interactions such as smiling, looking interested, remembering names, staying awake.

What is happening now is that, in response to our customers voting with their feet, we conventional doctors are re-learning all that stuff in postgraduate courses. I myself have a PhD in nodding

sympathetically and I presented a dissertation on fifty different ways of saying 'good morning' nicely (except I nearly failed in my oral when my examiner said 'good afternoon' and I didn't know what to reply. I mean, I'm a specialist, aren't I? Yes).

So, there is clearly a valuable lesson for us conventional chappies to learn from our alternative colleagues, crawl crawl slime slime slime, and it can only help all of us in doing what we really want, i.e. helping our patients in the best way possible and maybe getting famous as well.

In addition to the humane aspects, alternative medicine has some pretty powerful proponents and patrons. One of them is a person whose name I will not mention but whose identity I will hint at by saying that when his mum stops doing what she's doing, he'll be King of England. It is unclear precisely why this person is such a strong fan of alternative medicine, but I feel that this kind of broad commonsense view of health issues is precisely what this country needs – and PS my CBE hasn't arrived yet, though I sent in all the box tops last February.

However, despite all the obvious psycho-social advantages of alternative medicine, does it cure diseases? In other words, *does it actually work*?

Well, there's no point in asking me, is there? I mean, I'm The Enemy, aren't I? I mean, it's like asking the President of Coca-Cola whether Pepsi-Cola is actually nicer-tasting, isn't it?

Anyway, it doesn't matter because I shall now consider many of the alternative medicine techniques individually and let you judge for yourselves.

Please consult your own doctor before reading any further.

High Colonic Irrigation

For many years when I was young I used to see adverts on the back of the *New Statesman*, which was a kind of newspaper in those days, advertising High Colonic Irrigation. I must say that I visualised something like the Tennessee Valley Authority – or maybe Mesopotamia – bringing needed water to the parched valley of High Colon etc.

The truth is more bizarre, but less picturesque. It is based on the idea that – oh you know what it's based on, you just want to see me get embarrassed and coy, don't you? Anyway, for every Keynesian who believes that a good throughput is the mark of a good economy, there are two sceptics who uphold the law of diminishing returns and five opportunists who know where there's muck there's brass. The defence rests.

Rolfing

Rolfing is actually a serious alternative practitioner's discipline, and is all based on the belief that many diseases are caused by bad posture exaggerated by the effects of gravity, which I suppose might be true in certain circumstances, e.g. if you're drunk or shot. Anyway, practitioners who practise rolfing (known as 'rolfing contractors') do a sort of deep massage 'to loosen certain muscles and fascia and free the emotions and the mind'.

Actually, I had a cousin from out of town who used to do that sort of thing and she got 18 months, but then she didn't know she was rolfing, did she? Anyway, rolfing can be performed on a part-time or full-time basis and there are annual displays and exhibitions (e.g. the Pro–Am Rolf Championships). You have to be careful not to confuse ordinary rolfing with 'rolfharrissing', which is Australian and much less tasteful, although in some bizarre way I suppose you could think of it as an alternative to health.

Shiatsu

Shiatsu, like acupuncture, is based on traditional oriental medicine and is fervently supported by many people who can relate to something mysterious and totally unintelligible, provided it's oriental. These are the same people who are ready to believe in ginseng but not Horlicks, in Rabindrinath Tagore but not Desmond Morris, in bad karma but not bad moods, and in yin and yang but not Marks and Spencer.

Well, shiatsu scores heavily on the mysterious oriental scale, let me tell you. It's all based on the technique of applying pressure to one part of the body in order to produce an effect in another part (similar techniques are in use in the Western world, e.g. strangling). Thus, if you have a pain in your gall-bladder, the shiatsu doctor will apply pressure to 'the outside of your leg from the pelvis to the knee'. Though my manual doesn't say which leg – I suppose it depends on whether you dress with your gall-bladder to the left or right. In shiatsu teaching, the stomach is 'just to the outside of the front ridge of the shin-bone from the knee to the ankle', which sounds odd to non-orientals, but is actually the exact place where my stomach happens to migrate to on certain occasions, e.g. dentist's appointments or the morning after drinking half-a-bottle of sake.

Funnily enough, the shiatsu method doesn't say what to do to cure pain in the head – perhaps you're meant to apply shiatsu pressure to another part of the body entirely, e.g. your family doctor. More research is clearly needed here.

Bogus Doctors

I must admit that bogus doctors are not exactly recognised by anybody as genuine alternative practitioners, but that's an issue in itself. I mean if Alternative Practitioners grumble that *they're* not properly recognised by the regular Non-Alternative Practitioners (e.g. me and the Big Boys up the BMA), they can hardly complain if someone who isn't recognised as an Alternative Practitioner by *them* goes ahead and practises (in a fairly alternative way), without being recognised by any practitioners whatsoever. It's like being thrown out of the Association of Non-Conformists for not conforming to Association rules. And in real life, these bogus doctors often practise for ages without being recognised. Or caught. And what happens when they are caught? The moment they haul off some poor ex-invoice-clerk-who-always-wanted-to-be-a-doctor to court for having handled 35 women and tried to perform a few toe-nail removals, all his patients say how nice he was, and gentle, doctorly, authoritative and human.

We shouldn't put these guys in prison – we should employ them in the Health Service. For a start, they could teach medical students how to be nice and gentle, yet firm, authoritative and human (I'd teach those skills myself except I'm too busy using them to sell double-glazing in the evenings). Secondly, we could use them in Out-Patients. I mean, recent surveys have shown that 30% of all patients seeking medical advice haven't got a defined organic medical condition – which means, to one way of looking at things, that they're Bogus Patients. And we all know that doctors are absolutely awful at dealing with psycho-social problems (i.e. being nice to people who earn less than them), so why not employ a whole lot of proper Bogus Doctors to look after the Bogus Patients?

We could start a whole new Bogus College of Physicians which would issue proper 100% Bogus Diplomas (which have to be properly forged by accredited counterfeiters) and doctors, patients and Health Service would all benefit. We could probably pay them with genuine Monopoly money, which would not only solve a lot of funding problems but would also mean that they could get annual Monopoly pay increases as recommended by the Review Board – that would put them streets ahead of the rest of us ordinary doctors for starters. I believe that this suggestion of mine would bring alternative holistic humane medicine once more into the domain of the NHS, and would drastically reduce waiting-lists, patients' complaints, drug bills and unemployment in one bold and brilliant stroke.

Psychic Surgery

Psychic surgery is a fascinating form of therapy which has been categorised in the language of the transactional-phenomenological school of psychology as 'crap'. What happens in psychic surgery is that you go along to a psychic surgeon and he or she moves his or her hands over your body or, if you're too busy to attend yourself, over your photo or X-ray or wig or credit card or last school report. Using their special psychic powers they then 'divine' where the trouble is and what is causing it.

Now I have seen similar techniques used by other disciplines, e.g. plumbers and television repairmen, but I suppose the big difference was that they had dirtier overalls and charged more. Anyway, once the psychic surgeon has divined what is wrong, he organises the procedure known as psychic surgery. I don't know a lot about it myself, but I believe it's a pretty respectable sort of business with a proper psychic waiting-list and the option of going in a psychic side-room with private phone etc.

I'm told that one of the main advantages of psychic surgery is that you don't need to be anaesthetised (by a psychic anaesthetist) and it doesn't hurt ten days later when they take the psychic stitches out – though for the same money, why can't they use soluble ones?

Another advantage is that while the operation is being performed you (the patient) don't need to be there at all. Now think how helpful that could be for the NHS. I mean, all year round poor surgeons get hassled by executives who want their haemorrhoids fixed in August so they don't miss work – if we had psychic surgeons in the NHS we could do these guys' piles while they're actually working, so they don't even have to miss lunch. The only snag is that I don't know whether psychic surgeons ever do haemorrhoids, although I think I might be able to divine the answer if I just close my eyes and concentrate.

Phrenology

This is not actually a form of alternative medicine at all, but I thought we might start off on a fairly non-controversial note, otherwise there'll be tears before bedtime, you mark my words.

Phrenology was the science (if such it could be called) of diagnosing a person's talents and peculiarities by the shape and the bumps of their skull, or cranium, or, as we conventional doctors call it, head. The idea was that your personality inside your brain sort of pushed up from within and shaped the skull over it. Well, of course nowadays we know that in a few cases a personality with certain strong characteristics *can* alter the shape of your skull, e.g. a psychopath with an axe in Central Park after dark, but your own personality won't shift it a smidgeon. No sirree.

What phrenologists were good at was psychotherapy. They would place their hands on their customers' heads and make intelligent guesses about their lifestyle and personality by subtle clues – an expensive hairdo, a tiara, a Nazi helmet, things like that. And they would proceed by making exploratory statements which were bound to be true, e.g. 'there are two women in your life,' 'you care too much about things,' 'this'll cost you a florin', etc. And the interview would proceed depending on what the client replied, such as 'no, three' or 'no, I don't, I'm going to annexe Austria' and so on.

So really phrenology was a pseudo-science, a lot of hocus-pocus and mumbo-jumbo based on a minimal amount of slightly intelligent guess-work – the CIA is another example. Only when those guys feel your bumps, your bumps stay bumpy.

Homoeopathy

Homoeopathy is not like phrenology at all. Really it isn't. But the true scientific basis of the homoeopathic principle is not yet fully established, although it might be proven any decade now, and no thanks, I'm perfectly comfortable, I'm just shifting from foot to foot because there's a stone in my shoe and I always wring my hands like this when I'm talking about something complex and difficult to sort of, well, talk about.

What they do in homoeopathy is use very small doses of medicine. This is actually a very smart idea indeed since it has been shown that 10–30% of 'conventional' hospital patients suffer side-effects from drugs. If you use tiny doses of drugs, you'll have tiny side-effects.

What they also do is individualise each drug administration. This is also a very good idea. They look at you as a real person, your eye colour, your skin, your build, your credit-rating etc and pick the type and schedule of homoeopathic medicine accordingly. So it's not like conventional medicine, where you get ampicillin, £2.20, that's your lot, complete the course and who's next? In homoeopathy, you get ElizabethJonesicillin, it matches the colour of your eyes especially for you, with all our love and best wishes for a speedy recovery, £4.75 and call again soon.

There's something to be said for giving people less but giving it with more care and more heart.

Like this book, really. I mean a small dose'll probably do you just as much good as a big one.

Please read the next section, I write this only for you and I love you so much.

THE OCCULT & PARANORMAL

Along with the rise of alternative medicine and faith healing, has come a resurgent interest in the occult and paranormal. Perhaps a brief definition is in order at this point. The word 'occult' simply means 'hidden', and 'paranormal' applies to all phenomena that are deemed by society to be outside the bounds of what is considered the normal course of events, e.g. an SDP convention could be paranormal but never occult. As a matter of fact the people next door are into mysticism and have named their eldest son Paranorman. And you can see why. Here are some cold scientific facts.

Telekinesis

Telekinesis is the term given to the power of the brain to move objects without touching them. Since there is no such thing as telekinesis, it's a bit of a waste of a word as far as I'm concerned, but I suppose the language has got lots of words for things that don't exist in reality, e.g. unicorns, SDI, democracy etc. Anyway, the idea behind telekinesis is that there are supposed to be people who can move external objects without direct contact and excluding obvious tricks, like turning lots of heads by shouting, 'Look at that naked woman behind you' and similar.

The theory is that the human brain is really like one of those remote-control gadgets for televisions, only without the battery and the little red light to tell you when it's working. The proponents of telekinesis have lots of examples, such as people who can heat up thermometers or make little boats scud around on a bowl of water, except they can never quite manage it when anyone's looking.

Could there possibly be such a thing as telekinesis? No, there couldn't. This is because the brain works on incredibly low voltage electricity – about one four-thousandth of the voltage needed for a pen-torch. And quite often there isn't even enough voltage to get the thinking done properly, let alone enough to telekinese a teaspoon or boil an egg out there. Now, some proponents of telekinesis say that it isn't electricity at all but some completely unknown force which affects the physical world in a way as yet completely uncharacterised and about which absolutely nothing is known. This argument is always possible, and husbands have used it to explain the lipstick on their underpants.

It is, of course, absolutely impossible for anyone, e.g. me, to prove absolutely that absolute nonsense is absolutely nonsense. However, there's no doubt that if you want to move a little boat by thinking about it hard enough, eventually you will – after all, that's how I won the Booker prize, seduced Sigorney Weaver, and bought my first three yachts at Cap Ferrat. And wrote this book. Or is that just fantasy?

Metempsychosis

Metempsychosis is an extraordinary word and an extraordinary phenomenon. But perhaps the most extraordinary aspect of all is that, on the one occasion when I was playing Scrabble and somebody made 'psychosis', I had two M's and two E's to go in front of it but no T! Call it coincidence if you like, but I think that Dark Forces were at work and I said so plainly to my opponents – a couple of doctor-friends of mine called Faustus and Caligari. Anyway, what metempsychosis means (apart from about eighty points, if you can land on the double-word-score square) is the transmigration of the soul. The idea is that when you die your soul flits about and then settles into the body of something else, a bit like a spiritual version of musical chairs.

But there are a couple of things that bother me. Firstly, what happens if the supply of bodies is all used up and there's nothing for your soul to hop into when you finally pop your clogs? Is there a sort of clearing agency for disembodied souls like a celestial Central Casting ('Nothing for you today, Mr Pythagoras, though we may have a Brazilian taxi-driver going free tomorrow')?

And secondly, what was the recipient-body or landlord-body doing *before* the migrant-soul (or tenant-soul) metempsychosed into it? I mean, here am I, with the body of a perfectly normal (or nearly) NHS doctor. Now, is the soul inside me *already* a second-hand one that used to be Vercingetorix or Guy Fawkes or Joan Collins or a cat run over in Marrakesh or whatever? Or is the soul inside me *really* mine and just waiting to be loosened when I slip off the twig, so it can roost inside Michael Jackson or (preferably) Jamie Lee Curtis or half a pound of Viennese salami or such? Or is it possible that I have no soul at all and am merely an empty body waiting for a soul to occupy it – just as my wife always says, particularly at weekends? More research is clearly needed here.

Extra-sensory Perception

Actually, one of the greatest proponents of the theory of extra-sensory perception was a bloke I once met called Hubert Fraffleigh-Dymne (pronounced 'Frightfully Dim'). Hubert tried to train as a paratrooper but was thrown out – well, they all are, aren't they, that's how they train them! Arf arf arf, sorry, it must have been that Tia Maria at supper. Anyway, Hubert was dismissed from the regiment after a training exercise when he was dropped behind enemy lines in Uttoxeter and misunderstood his instructions, so that he buried his sealed orders and swallowed his parachute. And having failed at paratrooping, Hubert got fixated with everything that began with 'para'. He took a correspondence course in para-psychology and the paranormal, bought a villa in Paraguay and drank nothing but paraffin.

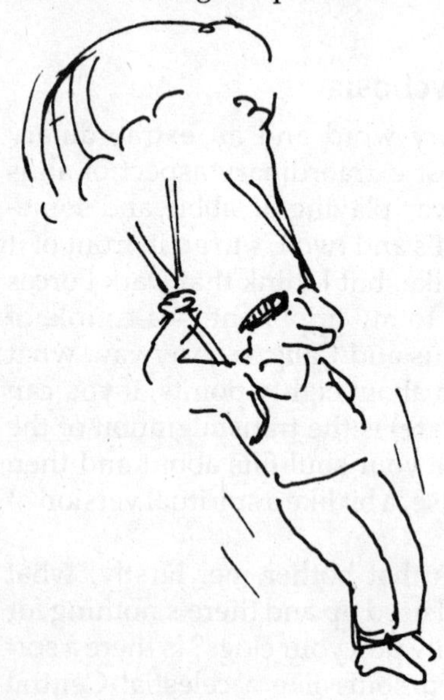

Anyway, according to Hubert, brains could communicate directly with each other by ESP without needing speech or language (or the phone), which was just as well in his case since he was so upper-crust he was totally unintelligible – even more when he started on the paraffin (mostly it interfered with his speech because he kept on forgetting to spit out the wick).

Now, is there anything to ESP and the occult transmission of thoughts? I don't think so. It's similar to telekinesis in that some people seriously want to believe in it and have to call upon forces that are totally unknown to the real world and which cannot be measured or monitored (the National Security Council is another example). Let me ask you this – how can it be that human beings can understand each other's thoughts *without* speech when we all know that 99.997% of the time we don't understand what the other person is thinking even *with* speech, e.g. during a marriage?

The real issue here is that we human beings are infinitely more complex and subtle than we realise and vastly more capable of communicating without speech than even the highest order of non-human primate e.g. politicians. We convey a thousand thoughts, reflections and attitudes covertly in our body language, clothing, speed of movement and expression, lapel badges and personal small-arms. We don't need ESP to explain the way we transmit our thoughts. At least, I don't think so. Over and out.

THE DOCTOR TUNES INTO YOUR WAVELENGTH

Q:

A: No – haven't picked up a thing. I guess that proves there's no such thing as ESP in print.

Diseasesology

As a hard-working physician fully committed to the National Health Service even during times of stringency and cut-backs, I am aware that no doctor can successfully practise the art of medicine without an adequate supply of two things – diseases, and patients to bring them to the hospital. Ignoring the rising tide of hysteria and panic, I offer you here a complete list of those conditions with which the NHS has no difficulty coping, in the hope that if you're thinking of developing a disease you'll be a good citizen and pick one of these. Please bring this section of the book with you to the out-patient waiting room, where you can read it again. And again and again.

Dutch Elm Disease

Once the bane of the clinic and waiting-room, this embarrassing personal complaint is nowadays more of a nuisance than a threat. A poll of 30 top consultants in the busy South-East shows that at present there are no patients with Dutch Elm Disease (whether acute or chronic, plain, scaly, or morbilliform) on their waiting-lists.

It therefore seems that if you are suddenly struck down, it's 'full speed ahead and no waiting' for a hospital bed. In fact, it may be the quickest way in. *One cautionary note*: Do check the licence of the consultant. I mention it only because of the recent case of 'Cowboy Surgeon X' – the first emergency tree-surgeon in Stoke Newington to be struck off for malpractice during a hurricane.

Hangnail

More good news! Hospital waiting-lists for hangnail are at an all-time low! In fact, many highly trained hangnail surgeons have so much time to spare that they are now treating the commoner types of hangnail by re-attaching them rather than paring them off. Hangnail transplants may be just around the corner and there might soon be further exciting developments for hangnail-less couples.

Tiredness

Yes, a complete tiredness service is now available at *your* local hospital. After years of debate and argy-bargy, the NHS now has the technology which – let's be honest – is the envy of the world. In over 95 per cent of District General Hospitals, patients suffering from acute tiredness can actually be guaranteed *a minimum of three hours deep sleep*, undisturbed by interruptions or interventions of any kind.

To find your own local 'tiredness clinic', just follow the signs marked Casualty Department.

If the problem is more chronic and requires longer and more profound sleep, ask for the Out-Patient Transport Office.

Hypochondriasis

This 'Cinderella of the psycho-pathological family' is just waking up and wants to go to the ball! Never have the opportunities been better for the fully-committed and properly-trained hypochondriac. The waiting-lists of Britain are yours. Due to the multifarious nature of the symptoms of true hypochondriasis (not the 'pseudo-hypochondriasis' known as 'being ill'), it is now possible for each hypochondriac to be on seventeen waiting-lists simultaneously. These may include waiting-lists for gastroscopy, tonsillectomy, hip transplant, prostatectomy, debt rescheduling or ante-natal care.

Heatstroke

Current estimates of general medical wards show conclusively that there are as of 1 November *no patients with heatstroke in Britain's hospitals*.

This astounding achievement has taken many months, since the dangerous dark days of last July when heatstroke lurked around every corner. It is one example out of many to show what caring government can achieve.

Friday

Although not formally recognised by the International Committee on the Nomenclature of Diseases, there is conclusive evidence from the scientists of our fecund and productive research institutes that what we have previously called 'Friday' is actually a disease.

Virologists have isolated a sub-virion particle, with a 24-hour incubation period, which produces all the symptoms of 'Friday' in guinea-pigs and mice. They have code-named it 'Thursday'.

If you have the classic symptoms of 'Friday' – extreme thirst, inability to concentrate, neurasthenia, lassitude, longitude, etc – then make an appointment with your doctor straightway. Before you realise it, it'll be next Wednesday – or even the Wednesday after that – and your 'Friday' will be in remission.

Don't thank me it's just part of the Service!

EBV – THE YUPPY PLAGUE

The shadow of a new viral infection has cast its pall over the finest of the West's crop and threatens to extinguish their light with a seething cauldron of medical symptoms, hysteria and the ever-present Damoclean sword of mixed metaphors.

Yes. The name of the beast is the **Epstein-Barr virus**, known among the cognoscenti – who are proud to number me as among those whom they exclude – as **EBV**. The virus was discovered by the eminent scientists Epstein and Barr, who claim that they didn't build it themselves, but just found it. Precisely who left it wherever they found it, and precisely why they didn't take it to Lost Property or inform The Authorities is a matter of much speculation.

Either way, Epstein and Barr discovered it, patented it, bred it and now join the immortal teams of collaborative scientists, such as Banting and Best (insulin), Sabin and Salk (polio vaccine), Burke and Hare (necromancy), Marks and Spencer (underwear), Gilbert and Sullivan, Aston and Martin, etc, etc.

The Epstein-Barr virus is the cause of a condition known as glandular fever, more correctly called 'infectious mononucleosis'. The name was officially changed in 1969 in order to provide doctors with a diagnosis with enough letters to fill the bottom line of sick certificates, leaving no space for forgers to add things like 'may die Friday' or 'of the worst kind' to get them an extra week off.

However, all that is by the by. Infectious mononucleosis is, as its name suggested, a contagious – or infectious – condition in which the patient experiences all the classical and obvious symptoms of becoming mononucleotic. Clear so far? Good.

Well, infectious mono was one thing, but now there is another silent infection with EBV in which the patient *doesn't* know he is ill until *afterwards*. Scary, no? The patient gets the illness and doesn't know it, and then having got better from something which he didn't know he'd got, suddenly feels worse which is actually a symptom of getting better compared to a time when he really felt well. And now doesn't. It's a worry, isn't it?

What happens is that the patient gets a 'post-viral syndrome' composed of malaise (the correct word for feeling like a dishcloth that's served two years' hard labour on a British Rail buffet-counter), lethargy, neurasthenia, myalgia (which means pains in the muscles, as opposed to youralgia which means nothing at all) and depression. Now this cluster of symptoms – known as a syndrome in order to fool the lay-press – is fairly widespread anyway. In order to qualify for the condition of 'EBV post-viral syndrome', you have to have all of these symptoms (a) on a day other than Monday when everyone has them anyway, and (b) an income of £30,000 or more. Otherwise you're just lazy. Right. Now let's see how this virus is spread.

EBV – Mode of Transmission

Detailed and meticulous research has been done by myself and my team at the Centre for Research into Communicable and Broadcastable Diseases plc (A Division of Medicine Balls Worldwide Inc). There is now no doubt that the virus originated in Islington where it bred in the upper respiratory tract (= up the nose in polite lingo) of 'Patient Zero' who alleges that he 'worked' in advertising. The virus bred during the summer of 1983 in a warehouse of damp Filofaxes which provided it with all the nourishment and dividers that it needed to divide.

There is now unequivocal evidence that the virus is transmitted by oral contact over cellular car-phones. And it breeds in home pasta-makers and espresso coffee-machines. It also seems that the virus can undergo a 'dormant' phase, during which it can lie latent but still multiply and divide. It does this inside any machine that has an alpha-numeric key-pad particularly under the 'multiply' and 'divide' keys and even more particularly if the device is 'credit-card thin' and does things like beep on your wife's birthday and do currency conversion.

EBV – How Can You Avoid It

Do not panic. You can avoid this serious condition if you follow these simple steps.

1. Do not speak to anyone on your car-phone until they have had a blood-test.
2. NEVER, NEVER, NEVER share someone else's Filofax. (Aside from EBV infection, it is also a way of introducing major problems such as remembering their wedding anniversary instead of yours, calling your children by the wrong names, etc, etc.)
3. Burn all calculators and pocket computers or take them to your doctor to get them sterilised.
4. Now panic.
5. Join a well established Health Maintenance Organisation such as Medicine Balls Ecumena Health Inc, which will dispose of your electronic apparatus for you and give you a letter to take to the office.
6. Take the rest of the day off.
7. Under no circumstances should you believe any of the scare-stories and 'how to avoid EBV' advice that you read in the newspapers or books.
8. Particularly this one.

Doctorology

Whilst the National Health Service is clearly committed to the fight to eradicate disease and suffering, it is also clearly committed to the eradication of other social problems, particularly doctors. As a result, many of us practising physicians have sent pathetic photos of ourselves to the World Wildlife Fund and have been granted status as an endangered species plus two visits a year from Princess Anne.

Yet it is clear to me that many of the public do not understand the nature of the doctor species and its variants. Some people do not know, for instance, the difference between a houseman and a houseboy. The answer is, by the way, that a houseboy is chosen for his looks and is better paid. Here is a user's guide to the various kinds of doctors that there are, including nurses.

DOCTORS

The Houseman

The houseman is the bottom of a heap which is composed entirely of people who remember exactly what it was like when they were at the bottom, but who have put on a lot of weight as they've clambered upwards. It's actually very difficult for me as a doctor, albeit an exalted and renowned one, to explain to my lay readers (albethey exalted and renowned ones, grovel, lick, toady, slurp-slurp) what it once felt like to be a houseman. But I'll try.

Mostly, it was like being a galley-slave in *Ben Hur* in the bottom row of a trireme. Or rather, it was like being the bloke that washes the underwear of the galley-slaves in ditto ditto ditto. As a houseman, you feel as if you know nothing except what your superiors tell you, which is mostly that you know nothing. You have power over nothing and responsibility for everything, like the Minister in Charge of Earthquakes, or Denis Howell, in the days when we had one of those.

You have to know everything about your patients e.g. allergies, fads, blood pressure, size of liver, war record, innermost unfulfilled fantasies, sock size, etc. And as if that wasn't bad enough, you're in servitude to your consultant (see below, but look up while doing so) who is probably an autocratic old bastard and you're expected to know everything about *him*, e.g. fads, allergies, size of liver, wife's birthday, mistress's birthday, war record, mistress's war record etc.

As regards rank, status and dignity, you have none. Your place in the scheme of things is such that even the hospital cockroaches will get their own personal space in the staff car-park before you do. In the great ceremonial parade into Christmas dinner you walk in behind the matron's cat. The only people in the world that you can look down on are drug reps. And psychiatrists. Oh, and the patients of course.

Without going into boring 'when I was a houseman' stories, I'd just like to say that when I was a houseman I was on call one night in two and paid £108 a month (half my hourly rate as a baby-sitter). And why did I do it? Why did I persevere and slave in the service of medicine and mankind? Well, because like all young doctors, deep in my heart I had a burning desire to be the leader of the Social Democrats, of course.

But it certainly wasn't all misery. There was camaraderie; there were girls and there were women and sometimes there were nurses, too (this was before Griffiths); there were parties and minor short-lived bacchanalia, gasps of passion, desperate mouths seeking another, and hurried intimate fumblings – and all that just to get a cup of tea at the League of Friends cake-stall.

Recently, a young student listening at my knee (we can't afford chairs in my teaching hospital) asked me, as I recalled these vivid scenes, whether I'd do it again if I had the chance. With a twinkle in my wise old eye, I chuckled and said that I'd rather do the splits on a barbed-wire trampoline.

The Senior House Officer

If the medical hierarchy can be compared to a tribe (and believe me it can – with cannibalism, massacres, blood feuds and the whole schmeer), then the Senior House Officer (SHO) is like the pubertal man-child.

The name is a misnomer and part of the out-dated military flavour of the profession – like calling the common room the 'Doctor's Mess', which is admittedly less of a misnomer. Anyway, the SHO is what you become after your houseman year. It's like a sort of purgatory in that it still scares the blazes out of you, but it's better than hell. You're still pig ignorant, but you have one factor in your favour that endears you to the older, more desperate members of the nursing profession, i.e. you're still alive and might make it to a marriageable age.

As time passes, you know a fact and then another. You learn a third fact, and then realise in a flash of insight that you've forgotten the first two. A week of burning the midnight oil and you re-learn the first two, of which one is now out-dated. You try looking after cases (or people if their diseases aren't interesting). You make a mistake and feel embarrassed. You make the same mistake twice and now you call it experience. You repeat it three times and now you can say, 'in case after case after case . . .'

All the time you are growing older. Soon it will be time to spin yourself a cocoon, to become a pupa, to dissolve your own self, thaw and resolve into your new form. Soon you will emerge from your chrysalis into the bright new dawn as the multi-coloured and fully-fledged maggot we call . . .

The Registrar

The registrar is the wonderfully wise young man who knows all the answers, but hasn't yet learned which are the important questions. (All this pseudo-philosophising of mine is utter and total cobblers by the way – my doctor says it's all a side-effect of my hay-fever tablets. Sorry.)

The registrar stands on the threshold of Learning, with his hand on the doorknob of Knowledge, his eye on the physiotherapist of Temptation, his lips on the backside of the Establishment and his signature on the . . . on the mortgage of . . . erm . . . His New House. Yes, well. For this is the Age of the Getting of Wisdom, when he shall become no stranger to research, and shall be found amidst dusty old tomes or else consulting the sayings of ancient sages as they clarify the mysteries of the occult, e.g. the 3.30 at Kempton Park.

At this stage of your career, you can begin to show an interest in some form of specialising. With luck, you can suck up to some consultant in some rarefied speciality and think of some immensely useful question that needs to be answered, e.g. the relationship between long-sightedness and the colour of your left parathyroid, or the chance of successful hernia surgery if your brother-in-law is an MP, etc.

And then you take some extra exams to get more qualifications and half the alphabet traipsing after your name. And the future looks bright and you want to discover the cure for something – the common cold maybe, or perhaps halitosis, or even boredom. Then, just as you're zooming down the runway and approaching V2 and take-off, along come the economic cut-backs and suddenly your only chance is if you want to specialise in diseases of Channel Tunnel workers. At the end of which the light appears very dim indeed, and the only fate awaiting you is that of being a consultant, which is what I shall tell you about soon, if the tablets wear off in time.

Nurses

Several of you have written to say that you have spotted in many hospitals and clinics a rather different kind of doctor, the kind that wears frilly arm-bands, black stockings and lacy hats. Well, we insiders tend to call that kind of doctor 'peculiar', mainly because dressing up like a nurse is a really bizarre thing to do, unless you are a nurse. Even then, some of those funny hats make even Carmen Miranda look unassuming.

I recently conducted a poll in which 17,000 members of the public (or friends of ditto) were asked to arrange the 100 most difficult jobs in the world in order of difficulty. Amazingly, the job of nursing came equal third – lagging behind the jobs of diving for natural pearls in New Bond Street and stalking roebuck on the M40, and tying for third place with Enriques Ramon, who is Baby Doc Duvalier's estate agent.

For all practical purposes, nurses have the hardest, the most wearing and the most exhausting job in the NHS, with the possible exception of the patients. The point is that the entire focus of a nurse's life is looking after sick, demanding, frightened people with a wide range of mental or physical problems, i.e. doctors. Nurses get trained in biology, physics, practical electronics and psychology; are ready at any moment to defibrillate an arrested heart; compress a severed artery; wipe a bottom; brush away a tear; or make a cup of tea (the last three tasks usually performed for a houseman).

And for these Herculean tasks their pay and standards of living have almost always been so rotten that marrying a doctor seemed almost attractive by comparison. In the days when I was a Junior Registrar (way back in the dawn of 1980), nurses were paid roughly the same as the daily take of a parking-meter in the West End. Now things are different – parking-meters do much better.

I honestly don't know what the Griffiths report will actually do for the future of nursing – perhaps, what the British Navy did for the future of the dodo. But, in my opinion, nurses are, on the whole, the most dedicated, successful and outstanding group of professionals anywhere in the United Kingdom. And will therefore probably be sold to the Americans next week.

Cardiologists

Cardiologists are heart doctors. Unlike nurses they do not have to wear frilly hats and armbands. They wear a different kind of uniform – usually a subtle, thin-stripe, grey suit and matching facial expression. They are not the same as heart surgeons in that nobody showed them how to do surgery. This means they have to pretend that they could do it if they wanted to, but don't want to, because it's soppy, so there.

Cardiologists use a thing called a stethoscope through which they listen to the heart – an activity that is called 'auscultation' in order to make the patients think that the doctor is doing more than just listening to the heart. By listening to the sounds that the heart makes, a cardiologist can detect all kinds of problems, such as stenosis of the mitral valve, calcification of a biscuspid aortic valve, deposits of carbon on the plugs or bent tappets. It takes nearly nine years to train and believe me you need six of those just to work out which of the heart sounds is 'lub' and which one's 'dub'. Come to think of it, I'm not sure why you need to know, unless it's to ask a surgeon to cut one of them out. My best friend Dave wanted to be a cardiologist and turned up for his first day on the coronary care unit to look after a Very Important Cabinet Minister who'd had a heart attack, and the consultant said, 'How good are you at listening to soft muffled sounds and making sense of what you hear?' Dave replied very good, and the consultant said, 'Then you can ring for the Minister's taxi.'

But that experience didn't put Dave off at all; he slaved and studied for another eleven years and trained under the best doctors in the field, and now he's Shadow Minister for Transport in the SDP and gets taxis for everyone.

Cardiac Surgeons

Cardiac surgeons are unutterably glamorous and brave and wonderful and specialise in dashing around and buckling their swashes, like a medical equivalent of Indiana Jones (with the thoracic cavity playing the part of the Temple of Doom).

Generally speaking, they do not lack self-esteem or pride in their

work, and one of them said that if the human body was like a motor-car, his job was changing the spark-plugs with the engine still running. Not to be outdone, a cardiologist (i.e. non-surgeon type, see above) said that *his* job was even worse because he wasn't allowed to lift the bonnet, and could only listen to the engine, sniff the exhaust fumes, check the ash-trays and then add digoxin to the petrol.

Cardiac surgeons have at least three options open to them. They can perform open heart surgery, closed heart surgery or (on Thursday afternoons) early closing heart surgery. In open heart surgery, the patient's circulation is kept going by a pump (probably an American one, dash it all) and the heart flops about like a twitching, palpitating fish, just like when you're in love for the first time, only this time someone's holding it. And slicing it open, come to think of it.

Open heart surgery is altogether a very upmarket, yuppy, A1-B1 kind of surgery, performed on people who have big BMWs by people who have bigger BMWs. You've probably seen this kind of surgery on the telly. The patient is anaesthetised after being checked for cardiac function, ventilatory capacity and credit status. Then he (usually a he, because heart disease only partly participates in Equal Opportunities Programmes) is connected to a ventilator and the by-pass pump-and-oxygenator, which are complex machines that go FWTHUMPP-P'TISSSS, and cardiac output monitors, which go FNEEP-FNEEP-FNERRRP-BIP if all is well, or MNEEEEEEEEEN if they are broken or the patient is dead. Then a whole lot of things happen under the drapes to do with bits of gristly stuff and slippery mushy substances (this is just to get the patient's pyjamas off, mind you). Next, the surgeon opens the heart, removes the bit that isn't

THE DOCTOR ANSWERS YOUR QUESTIONS

Q: I used to suffer from megalomania, but I cured myself by sheer will-power and concentration. In fact, I think I've done an amazingly brilliant and stunningly clever job in controlling this tendency. Don't you agree?

A: Yes, you're the most famous cured megalomaniac in the whole world. Now, could you get out of my light please, I'm trying to write a book?

Q: Will you mention me in the book?

A: No.

working, or is broken, and replaces whatever he has to. Then he wakes the patient up and gives him a receipt for the bit he's taken out.

It's a highly thrilling, demanding and exciting business (particularly for the doctors, less so for the patients) and I think that if you asked most cardiac surgeons why they did it, they'd say it was for the betterment of mankind, the alleviation of suffering and the thrill of using machines that go FWTHUMPP-P'TISSSS. And who can blame them?

MEDICAL JOURNALS

As I sit here cogitating the profundities of the human condition in my book-lined study (I lined it with a book when I ran out of wallpaper), I realise that we doctors read different things to you humans. We read medical journals and research papers and stuff. We don't read *Penthouse* or *Playboy*, we don't have time (so we just look at the pictures). But, to you members of the public, medical journals may be a bit of a closed book. Here then is a survey of the most important constituents of our medical esoterica.

Letters

The letters section of our medical journal provides the necessary forum for a frank, free and earnest exchange of prejudice and invective. Doctors are, it goes without saying, above an exchange of mere personal insult. But they lower themselves to it from time to time on the basis that it's a bit like a high-fibre diet for the soul – and lots of things, however unpleasant, are 'better out than in'.

Characteristically, the most insulting letters begin with a cringing, grovelly note that ushers in the body blow. Say, for instance, a Dr Fossington is writing in to disagree with a previous article. He might write something like:

> Whilst I would agree with Schmaltz, Endelbaum, Huppert and Klotz (Feb 19) that some aspects of ulnar tenosynovitis ('Adulterer's Elbow') are controversial, it is quite apparent to anyone with even the most elementary grasp of the problem that the Schmaltz hypothesis, although superficially attractive to the uneducated reader, is unfounded, untenable, specious, fallacious, erroneous, incorrect, false and, in every important aspect, misleading and full of crap.
>
> It has been repeatedly shown (Fossington and Smythe 1961) that the incident of adulterer's elbow depends on the length of the elbow itself (Fossington, Smythe and Cross 1969), the development of ulnar exostoses (Fossington, Fossington and Cross 1971) and the frequency of adultery (Fossington and Kashoggi 1971, 1972, 1973 [three times], 1975 and 1979). That our major contributions in this field should have escaped the notice of the authors is expected from such a motley bunch of poxy air-heads that couldn't tell an ulnar diathesis from a thrombosed haemorrhoid.

Etc etc. This kind of stuff is the very lifeblood of modern medicine – i.e. it's somebody else's and it's spilt freely. And what your busy and overworked doctor reads after the letters, are the . . .

Obituaries

Of all the sections of the medical journals, the obituaries are invariably the best written and most widely read. There is a peculiar literary pleasure and reward in reading the glowing eulogies and euphemisms after the death of a Grand Old Physician – perhaps it's the innermost artist in all of us appreciating the fact that the dreaded old bugger is actually dead at last.

But, my dears, the language! As Oscar Wilde once so neatly didn't put it, 'There are lies, damned lies and obituaries.' I mean the way the ever-so-recently deceased are praised you'd think that if they'd managed to hang on to life for another fortnight all British illness would have been eradicated. All deceased medics, according to the obit columns, are a bunch of saintly, dedicated, super-human, lily-white water-walkers – contrasting sharply with the living docs pilloried in the correspondence section, who are a bunch of clay-footed, thick-skinned, numb-skulled, hare-brained buffoons.

I can't quite work out how it happens that a doctor can be humiliated and vilified in a letter on one Friday, and then be transformed posthumously into a hybrid of Pasteur, Fleming and Schweitzer by the next Friday. Maybe there are two entirely different populations of doctors – the bastards in the letters section and the angels in the obituaries section. In which case, which is the group that looks after all the patients? (Please send me your answer to this vital question – I need to know).

But in the meantime, for your edification and use – should you ever need to read a medical obituary, or even write one about a dedicated healer, compassionate clinician, inspiring teacher or obstreperous old git – here is the key to what the words mean.

Medical Obituaries – A Glossary

Derek loved life: Derek got drunk often
Jocelyn lived life to the full but always made time for his family: Jocelyn got drunk often and quarrelled with his wife
Charles did not tolerate fools gladly: Charles was a psychopath with a foul temper
Charles was a man of incisive wit who did not tolerate fools gladly: Charles was a psychopathic surgeon with a foul temper
Despite his many commitments: despite his extensive private practice
Well-known as a moderator and voice of reason: indecisive
Eminent in the corridors of power: a creep
Always had time for colleagues and friends: Couldn't find any work to do
Something of an enigma: mad
Wide range of interests: lecherous

Much-loved by ward staff and colleagues: adulterous
Never lost his enthusiasm for neurology/immunology/Julie Andrews: boring monomaniac
Maintained a sense of youthful enthusiasm: watched *The Muppets* regularly and had a tantrum when he couldn't get his way
Always known as 'C.G.' to friends and colleagues: pompous old duffer who might, or might not, have forgotten his own name
Familiar figure in the corridors of St Nissen's: could never find his way back to his office
Never lost his common touch: swore a lot
Never forgot his origins: maintained a Northern accent and Brylcreemed hair
A well-rounded human being: played golf three afternoons a week
Roguish sense of humour: no sense of humour
Sorely missed by his family: under-insured

Drivingology

It has been suggested that the human mind and the act of driving a car are mutually incompatible, and this has been backed up by hundreds of social psychologists (who are the worst drivers of all). Speaking personally, I think the standard of a person's driving relates directly to their personality and as a compassionate, empathic and sensitive doctor, I drive like a speed-crazed blood-hungry disinhibited psychopath. Perhaps the question I am asked most commonly about psychology and driving is 'Did you know you were doing 90mph in a built-up area?' Since I have found that looking at the speedometer is bad for my blood-pressure, I can honestly answer 'No'.

In this timely review of the social framework of driving and the driver, I shall examine the major conflicts between health and motoring, concluding with a few remarks concerning the impact of motoring on pedestrians.

MOTORWAY MADNESS

Is there such a thing as motorway madness? Yes, there is. Oh good. Well, actually we use the phrase 'motorway madness' to describe a particular form of crowd behaviour or herd instinct in which inhi-

bition levels and normal, cautious restraints are down-regulated by contradictory environmental factors culminating in sensory deprivation, perceptive signal-noise defects, narrow analogue-performance margins and excessive de-skilling parameters, i.e. a mile of roadworks in fog on the M6. So, in some respects, if you do have an accident, it's not completely your fault because we as a *society* are partly to blame.

It's the social objectives of our whole culture that set a frame in which individuals are simply the Skinnerian pawns of ritualised aggression-ventilation. Thus, if there was natural justice, it would be the M6 which would be perceived as the aggressor and found guilty of having got up and hit the motorist out of spite, and the driver would be simply closed for re-surfacing. (By the way, if you have had an accident, do give this article to your lawyer – it may not get you off, but at least he'll have a laugh, so one of you will be in a good mood after court.)

So then, what is the basis of this over-crowding herd behaviour? Well, the most famous investigations into this problem were done by the Trossachs' behaviouralists, McPhee, Fye, Faux and Phumm. They trained one group of guinea-pigs to operate car-simulators under high stress (e.g. threat of castration, evisceration, watching the new Bruce Forsyth series etc). Then they trained another group to avoid any form of loneliness and isolation. Then they anaesthetised seven-eighths of all the guinea-pigs' brains and turned them loose in Metros on the M1. The guinea-pigs showed exactly the predicted response. They displayed a sense of reckless abandon, disregard for personal safety and covert suicidal tendencies – and every one of them drove into a Happy Eater and ordered the mixed grill.

However, that is not the only way in which motorways can condition human behaviour – it can be a force for good, rather than evil. For instance, at the Hove Everglades Hospital in the Barney Hayhoe Memorial Prostate Research Unit, senior scientists have invented a cure for prostatic hesitation (a condition known to urologists as 'trouble with the waterworks'). They cure it by simply showing the patients a photo of a sign saying: NO SERVICES ON MOTORWAY FOR 30 MILES. The treatment is extremely effective but there is one side-effect – 15% of the patients get car-sick.

PSYCHOLOGY AND THE LAW

Many modern philosophers have noticed that something bad happens to a man when he gets out on to a fast-moving motorway – particularly if he isn't in a car. Among these bad things is the sense of anomy, of lawlessness and lack of restrictions that may bring us into conflict with many authority figures, most of them policemen.

Why do we behave like that? Well, two traffic-psychologists at the University of Albuquerque (they were both former Roads scholars, actually) studied 200 policeman/driver interactions and concluded that the answer least likely to receive a friendly caution, when asked 'Where's the fire?', was 'In your eyes, officer.'

Transactional analysis of the ticket-giving process suggests that the speeding driver is challenging the sense of territorial insecurity of the policeman, who may be suffering from low self-esteem and ambivalence about his own gender identity, and that in handing out the ticket, he is symbolically taking revenge on his own mother for making him eat up all of his spinach.

This is why a very large number of psychologists in California respond to being ticketed by saying, 'I am not your mother and you don't have to finish your spinach if you don't want to.' The accuracy of this penetrating insight can be gauged by the fact that 82% of motorist-psychologists in California are either in prison or shot through the head. Which may be no bad thing for all concerned.

PHYSIOLOGY AND THE MOTORIST

In some way, everything we do in a car is symbolic, or reminiscent, of the way we do everything else in our lives – particularly when we were young and the car was the only place where 'everything else' was even a remote possibility. But what we fail to remember is that a car is moving (for some of the time), therefore some of the things we might do in it have certain consequences if we're meant to be driving at the time. For instance, it is well-known that motorway-driving lulls us into a sense of false security and detached contemplation, which some psychologists have termed 'sleep'. Obviously, this is potentially dangerous. But, unfortunately, ever-vigilant Mother Nature can adapt our reflexes even to these man-made hazards, e.g. we crash into something on the road, which immediately wakes us up. For those interested in preventive action, there is now available a very clever inertial-sensor which detects the movement of the head forward and makes a very loud noise in your ear. If you can't afford it, a mother-in-law may prove a useful substitute.

Finally, we use driving as a metaphor. We speak of an aggressive, ambitious man as having 'lots of drive'; we speak of 'driving force' and use the words 'sex-drive' (but only after the kids are in bed). In some respects, we are all travellers on a long road in a car which is not quite our own choice and design. We'd all like the Bentley on the Autostrada del Sol, but mostly, it's a 1978 Lada on the Exeter by-pass. Sic gloria mundi ever so slowly transit.

DRIVING IN AMERICA

Terrible things are happening on the highways of the United States, namely California. Motorists are getting frustrated and shooting and wounding each other in droves (or is the collective noun for maimed motorists 'drives'?).

I am reliably informed that at sites of altercations between motorists disputing, perhaps, the possession of the fast lane or trying to enter a solid stream of traffic at a 'Yield' sign, some irate persons have shown a slight tendency to bring out their shotgun and blast the disputee's head off his goddam shoulders.

Which could be regarded – at the very least – as 'driving without due care and attention', or maybe even 'failing to show consideration for other road-users'; unless your lawyer could convince the jury that the deceased had suffered from such a terrible migraine that what he'd really wanted all day was to have his head blown off his goddam shoulders and that the defendant was therefore showing him the greatest possible consideration.

Be that as it may, there is murder and mayhem on the motorway and even Californians are a mite worried about it – which is a real surprise for a state where an action like machine-gunning a dozen strangers in a shopping-mall tends to be regarded as valid social comment: *Like, hey, man, I think I can see where you're coming from.* (As a matter of fact, if you want my advice, I'd say every time you think you know where a weird Californian is 'coming from', you had best take cover until you're sure he's 'going back'.

Anyway, this Mad Max Motorway Madness has caused the emergence from the closet of a much-neglected, often-derided and endangered species, i.e. the Expert Psychologist. And it is he who has resurrected my favourite school of folk-lore bunkum, the psychology of spacio-temporal automobile interactions, i.e. car crashes.

CAR CRASHES AND SOCIETY

The Expert Psychologists have come to the conclusion that mankind is more capable of anti-social behaviour if personal contact is avoided and if personal identification is absent. For instance, they say, if you're walking along and you bump into someone on the pavement, you say, 'Oops, sorry!' and smile, whereas if you're driving and nearly bump into another car you honk your horn and you snarl. This is why – personally speaking – whenever I go shopping in London, I always make a point of driving on the pavement because you get much friendlier interactions that way. Particularly if you knock down a Californian psychologist.

Anyway, it seems that frustration has a very low threshold in a car because the means of communication are so limited. In ordinary life, for instance, we have graded responses for incidents from 'Oops' to 'Pardon' via 'Mind your backs!', to 'Excuse me', by way of 'Out of the sodding way!' right up to 'Let me through, I'm a doctor!' Whereas in a car you just have 'Honk.' Or, for the repetitive spirits amongst us 'Honk-honk.' Or if you're just a long-winded nerk, 'Honnnnnkkkkkk.' But it's not actually a language, is it? I mean, even geese can do better than that – in fact, with a fair command of honking, your average grey-legged goose can get himself properly mated, start a family *and* make his way to Greenland and back, whereas your average fathead in a Morris Marina with a honk twenty times as loud can't even get on to the A23 at Purley or shut his wife up. I mean, it goes to show, doesn't it?

Anyway, the Expert Psychologists point out that there are very few meaningful personal interactions that a driver can have – while he's driving anyway. With the right passenger, a quiet lay-by in the Chilterns and a full moon, you can manage quite a few meaningful interactions but that's another story. No, it isn't, it's the same story, because – according to the Expert Psychologists – the automobile and sex are irretrievably linked, not only in the lay-by, but also on the road and in the motorist's mind. And that's because the whole Californian schemozzle is yet another manifestation of the frustration of unexpressed sexuality of the American male. (I can't remember what the last one was – Donna Rice maybe).

YOUR CAR AND YOUR GENITALS

It seems that a man's car is actually a symbol of his genitals. Or rather what he'd like his genitals to look like, or do – which is an interesting thought, and one reason Californian psychologists give for not polishing the car while the neighbours are watching.

Anyway, your car is an external expression of your downbelows, and by the same token it seems that your garage is a symbol of your first playpen, a red traffic light is a symbol of your first experience of nappy-rash, a zebra-crossing is a symbol of Marmite soldiers and free milk, and a traffic warden is a symbol of your mother. Or (rarely) *is* your mother.

I don't know what a wheel-clamp is a symbol of – circumcision, possibly, except it's more expensive *and* more difficult to disguise. However, none of this explains what the average American male thinks he is doing with his car-qua-downbelows when he does something called 'tailgating', which involves sneaking up very close behind the car in front (latent automosexuality?), nor why it is that when he gets into an argument with another driver and gets out to settle any differences in a no-confrontational socially valid exchange of shot-gun fire, the other driver always turns out to be a Californian psychologist with bumper-envy.

More research is clearly needed on this important issue.

THE DOCTOR DEMONSTRATES HIS BREADTH

Q: I know this isn't your specialist subject, but I heard about this wonderful new James Clavell book which is a saga about three generations of Chinese businessmen who make an absolute fortune selling cuff-links and ear-rings and matching studs and stuff in Asia. They then take over the entire Chinese sub-continent with a chain of trinket shops running the length of the Great Wall, selling 5-carat accessories and knick-knacks. I don't suppose you know what it was called, do you?

A: I think it was *Tai-pin*.

Newfangledology

The atmosphere is all around us. But it is no longer the same atmosphere as previously (although maybe it never was). Anyway, all around us are signs of the victory of our advancing technology over the hostile forces of nature – radios, microwave ovens, phones, Zsa-zsa Gabor, etc. But can they do us harm? In the case of Zsa-zsa Gabor probably yes, but in the case of phones or radios probably not, unless you hear Zsa-zsa Gabor on either of them. Here is an analysis of the health hazards of our high-tech existence.

MICROWAVES AND OVENS

I must say I'm not exactly sure what *microwaves* are, but as I understand it, they seem to be a Japanese miniaturised version of electricity. In fact, like many scientists familiar with modern particle physics, I must confess that I don't completely understand the principles of a microwave oven, e.g. how to defrost chickens.

I seem to remember someone telling me that microwaves work on the same principle as an induction furnace in Physics O-level. Well, what happens in an induction furnace is that they have these huge magnets that keep on suddenly switching their polarity from North to South like opinion polls, only more reliable. This sets up changing magnetic fields inside the objects inside the furnace, e.g. aluminium scrap, bauxite, deceased business associates, etc. The rapidly-changing magnetic fields cause the material to melt, or at the very least to be unable to assist the police with their enquiries.

Now I don't quite know how similar a microwave oven is to an induction furnace, but I think that in theory if you could manage to stick your head into a microwave oven and turn it on, your fillings would explode. Mind you, your brain would have boiled two seconds before that, so you wouldn't even have time to worry about the cost of getting your teeth re-done anyway.

Now, the whole point is that microwaves are potentially very dangerous to delicate biological tissues and organs, e.g. chopped liver, smoked salmon, etc. But the most important question of all is: can the microwave damage your health in practice?

Well, the answer is NO, except in two circumstances – if you drop one on your foot, or if you are a hot-dog sausage. In fact, this damage was investigated in 1968 by the Italian biophysicist, E.

Pagliacci, in a set of experiments which would nowadays contravene the regulations of humane experimentation. Over a series of fifteen sessions, he exposed groups of mice and human volunteers to microwave ovens for up to three hours at a time. At the end of the course, the humans still couldn't heat a cup of soup, whereas the mice had learned to do soufflés and bouillabaisse and have now opened their own restaurant with rave reviews from every discriminating critic and Clement Freud.

The exact significance of these findings in terms of human physiology is still unknown.

NUCLEAR RADIATION

Nuclear radiation is very different from microwaves in that it is more likely to cause both somatic and genetic damage and to make stews and casseroles burn at the bottom. And all the way through, actually.

Nuclear radiation is caused by *atoms*, which are the smallest constituents of matter and of no significance unless they get together, just like ratepayers really. Some atoms are incredibly unstable (ditto ratepayers) and have *electrons* going round in high energy orbits that ought to be in lower energy orbits, where there's less stress and responsibility and the hours are better. Well, what happens is that these electrons eventually give in to peer-group pressure and go into a more blue-collar orbit, and the result is a bit like nature's version of a demarcation dispute: viz there is a large explosion apparently out of all proportion to the size of the initiating event.

Now much of the energy given off is in the form of *ionising radiation*, and I am reliably assured that this is the worst possible kind, though if you find yourself in a nuclear explosion, nobody seems to know which is the best kind of radiation. The Americans say theirs is. Nuclear radiation is so dangerous because it damages not only your skin and innards and bones etc, but also your *chromosomes*, which you should therefore try to cover up in the event of being radiated.

It has always puzzled me that in these days when a drug company can go to the wall for a rare side-effect in a useful product, somebody can make a thing that can wipe out an entire continent and all their grandchildren, and they don't even have to print a government health warning on it. Not that anyone would have enough time to read it anyway, I suppose.

So what protection is there in the event of nuclear radiation? Well, you will be pleased to hear that in the unlikely event of nuclear war, our Government plans to house us in bunkers twelve feet underground, lined with two feet of concrete and one inch of lead, and equipped with positive-pressure ventilation and ion-exchange fresh-water systems. The only drawback is that they are not going to be able to construct very many of these shelters in the four minutes available.

HEAT AND LIGHT

However unlikely it may seem, heat and light are actually different forms of the same *thing*, although, as the saying goes, objects that generate a lot of heat usually shed little light, e.g. Labour Party conferences. Mind you, not all heat is the same as light. There are actually three ways in which you can heat up an object – by *conduction*, by *convection* and by *radiation*. Or, if you prefer, you can use a ceramic hob.

Anyway, it is only *radiant* heat that is the same as light, as you can tell if you hold your hand close to the telly when Jeffrey Archer is on. These radiations are all forms of *electromagnetic rays*, and the parts of that spectrum that we can see we call 'visible light'. The parts that we can't see thus include things like ultra-violet, infra-red, trade deficits, social unrest etc, and we don't know much about those unless we hold a public enquiry.

Let's take *ultra-violet* first. It is a pure coincidence that our sun transmits ultra-violet rays at the same time as visible light because it's the ultra-violet that causes sun-tan. If they weren't transmitted together it could be dangerous, because you might get sun-tanned without realising it, e.g. at night. Of course, there are times when ultra-violet rays are *not* transmitted with visible light, e.g. this August.

In fact there are several different types of ultra-violet radiation – there is *Ultra-violet A*, which helps clear up some types of skin diseases, there is *Ultra-violet B*, which you get from sun-beds (possibly) and there are other miscellaneous ones, e.g. *Ultra-violet CB*, which lorry-drivers use, as well as radar and Channel Four. None of the others is associated with sun-tan unless you are a major share-holder.

At the other end of the spectrum is *infra-red* and this is the stuff you get from those funny glass-tube radiators and the older fancy ovens, which weren't microwave but which gave you hot-dogs that were cold on the outside and molten lead on the inside. As far as my adolescence was concerned, I always thought the way you felt afterwards was due to radiation sickness, but in fact it was mainly due to the ketchup.

THE DOCTOR ANSWERS YOUR QUESTIONS

Q: What are 'genitalia'?

A: People who work for the national airline of Italy.

TELEPHONES

Telephones have captured the imagination and the ear of mankind ever since the day that the famous scientist Alexander Fleming Bell made the first phone-call to his assistant Rodney Telecom and got his answering machine. But can they damage your health? Read on and find out (please reverse the charges if you're reading this long-distance).

Health Hazards of Telephones

Actually we doctors know a lot about the health hazards of telephoning, though of course we know much less about the hazards of getting through to the right number first time.

As a doctor myself – and a caring, sensitive parent of two young telephones and a Plan 4A with two extension sockets – I am often asked questions such as 'Hello, is that the Family Planning Clinic Hotline?'

Well, of course that's often a difficult question to answer, particularly at 1 a.m. on Saturdays, though I must say that, as a method of family planning, being phoned at 1 a.m. on Saturdays is as good as any.

For further information on this important subject you can read my major article in *Psychology for Yuppies* called 'The Phone As Bromide', or just give me a ring.

Anyway, we can split the main health hazards of phones into two groups – the hazards of using the phone to make calls, and the hazards of what happens when you get through to your friends, relatives, enemies, or (usually) completely random members of the British public.

Well, another question that many people ask me (after they've got over their disappointment that I'm not the Family Planning Clinic Hotline) is whether or not you can catch diseases from a phone handset. What they usually ask about is social diseases such as, you know, herpes of the ear-lobe (there was even a freak rumour in California about a new telephone-transmitted disease called Hearing-AIDS but sensible people didn't listen to it).

Of course, the answer is that NO, you can't catch social diseases from the phone, but everything is relative and I am willing to provide a letter on hospital notepaper saying that's where you caught it for a nominal sum. (A 'nominal sum', by the way, is a medical term meaning a sum nominated by a doctor.)

Be that as it is, there are certain medical conditions that one person can leave on a phone apparatus which *can* affect the next user. Garlic is a good example. It is the lingering odour of the previous user's breath that has allowed so many office phone-cleaning services to spring up, based on the rather mediaeval concept that the breath is a contagious source of diseases including malaria, bubonic plague, scrofula and halitosis.

Well, in all probability the only disease that is genuinely transmitted by the phone is the common cold and you might be able to avoid even that if you reverse the charges. From my long and detailed study of the use of the phone in the workplace, I would say they cause more trouble in other ways. Like when they transmit things far worse than bubonic plague, e.g. a further drop in oil prices, a request for a few bombers, the results of a by-election, etc.

In other words, many of the health hazards of the phone are due to the *psychology* of phoning, which is what we shall deal with next.

The Psychology of Telephones

The thing that's extraordinary about telephones is that, when we use them, we communicate using only our voice, omitting all other personal signals that we normally convey by non-verbal means (including body language, halitosis, herpes, etc – see above).

In fact, as mentioned by many great observers of twentieth-century life (such as Truffaut, Foucault and Groucho), there are major dangers in communicating solely with the disembodied voice. Mind you, without wishing to appear uncaring or insensitive in any way, I must say that I do have the occasional longing for the exact opposite of the disembodied voice, i.e. the disenvoiced body – Lorraine Chase would be a good start.

However, I digress. Many research psychologists have attempted to assess the stresses of using phones by devising an animal model of phoning. The most successful work has come from the Verona group of Carlo, Franco, Blanco, Bilko, Oxo and sometimes Zeppo. Working with a strain of laboratory-bred guinea-pigs using a specially modified pay-phone, they were able to show that 80% of guinea-pigs could be taught to dial, though the main problem was that they didn't have anywhere to carry their small-change. Further studies showed that 64% of guinea-pig calls got the wrong number first time, 20% of calls were used by guinea-pigs to try and sell life insurance or double-glazing, and 11% of the time their friends were out.

Phones in Planes

As the latest twist in the American way of making everybody feel paranoid and over-stressed, some airlines have put public phones in their aeroplanes.

Perhaps this is an idea that British Telecom could copy, simply in order to stop their phones being vandalised. Anyway, a recent survey showed that 19% of air travellers use the plane-phone during the course of a year, and that 97.2% of conversations consist entirely of statements about how amazing it is to be making this phone-call from a plane.

As part of my research into this banal and gimmicky advance in the communications industry, I myself attempted such a call recently. It was amazing.

Answering Machines

Recent theological research into the prophesies of the sixteenth-century seer, Nostradamus, has shown that answering machines were predicted and that they would be the plaything of the Evil One and the Ushers of Armageddon. And that's pretty much the way it's turned out.

Despite decades of use, no one has actually got used to answering machines and most people leave messages that begin 'Oh . . . ah . . . you're not in . . . oh . . . I can't get used to these machines . . . well, look . . .' etc, or else chicken out completely and then end up going round to your house and shouting abuse at the answering machine through the letter-box.

Actually, I have invented a brilliant technique to find out who is calling when I am in. I pick up the phone and speak in a very slow deliberate voice with bursts of crackly noise in between, e.g. 'Hello CHWARRK this is Robert Buckman speaking CHWURRR I am at home at the moment. If you wish to speak to me, please start talking after the tone. PLINNN.' Most people are flummoxed totally and say they'll call back later when I'm out. Tee hee.

Phone Sex

People have tried to explain the idea of phone sex to me, but I must admit that I really don't have a proper grasp of the subject at all.

Apparently, what happens is that you ring up some lady of easy virtue and she says rude things to you. As far as I can gather, it's the prostitute equivalent of Take-Away.

My only advice is that you should wash your ears carefully afterwards and never make this kind of call from a plane.

THE DOCTOR ANSWERS YOUR QUESTIONS

Q: Hello, is that the Family Planning Clinic Hotline?

A: No, it bloody well isn't, and do you know what time it is?

Psychologyology

Some have called the human mind 'the last unexplored frontier that comes after whatever it was that was the unexplored frontier before last'. And how true that is!

In this in-depth survey of matters psychological I take a penetrating look at the workings of the human mind: how to measure it, who should measure it and what colour it should be when it's finished. Then I move on to examine the fundamentals of human experience – the pain, the anxiety, the hysteria, the mortgage, etc.

YOUR IQ

Your IQ is your intelligence quotient, which means how intelligent you are compared with the average population as assessed by an IQ test. Since the only definition of 'intelligence' is the thing that's measured by an IQ test, you will immediately realise (unless you're not very intelligent) that it doesn't matter how stupid you think the test is, what really counts is how stupid the test thinks you are.

Actually, there are lots of different IQ tests devised by different

psychologists and the most important one was devised by the French scientist Binet. Which is awful because it means that if you fail on the Binet test you have the ignominy of being stupider than the average Frenchman. Though still smarter than the average French secret service agent. Or a bowl of *moules marinières*, come to that.

But before we get too depressed, we should remember that your IQ (of which the average is 100, and genius level 150) only says how intelligent you are and not how successful at your job or how happy a person you are. For instance, you could have an IQ of 75 and still be James Michener. Alternatively, you could have an IQ of over 100 and still work for the BBC (though this is less likely).

Some psychologists have in fact tried to correlate IQ with success at work, home and play, and the findings are pretty much what you'd expect. Thus, a survey of exclusive country clubs in Kent showed that most members of the leisured aristocracy had an IQ identical to their golf handicap. Or sock size, in the case of non-playing members. By contrast, the survey of stockbrokers yielded aggregated scores of between 130 and 140 (per firm).

Looking at Great Britain generally, the psychologists and sociologists found that the people with the highest IQs tended to be in their thirties, articulate, health-conscious, and tended to appear on Channel Four (or try to), to wear corduroy jackets (or try to) and to grow beards (or try to). As regards their profession or training, such people were usually found to be psychologists or sociologists who devised IQ tests and did surveys. When comparing several tests, the lowest scores on the Binet were found among doctors (who filled in the multiple choice boxes illegibly) and people called Eysenck.

THE PSYCHE – ANALYSTS, OLOGISTS & IATRISTS

As part of my in-depth research for this article, I went round to a well-known Medical Association (professional etiquette forbids me to mention which one, but I can hint that it was in Britain) and asked the commissionaire at the door to tell me the difference between psychologists and psychiatrists. He said the difference was about thirty quid an hour. For those of you who require more of the academic background to the two disciplines, drop me a line and I'll send you my bibliography and background reading, though actually I got most of it from my old *I-Spy Book*, Vol 61, 'At The Loony Bin' (in colour).

Anyway, my understanding of the world literature on the subject is that, according to psychologists, a psychologist is a scientist who has trained in various aspects of experimental psychology, neurophysiology, operant conditioning and interpersonal dynamics, whereas a psychiatrist is a doctor who couldn't keep up the payments on his stethoscope. Psychiatrists, on the other hand, tend to view the schism in a more allegorical style. Thus, according to a very senior psychiatrist (they come a bit cheaper when they're not so up-to-date), neurotics are people who build castles in the air, psychotics are people who live in them, while psychiatrists are people who charge them rent, and psychologists are like Men From The Council who come round once in a blue moon, talk incomprehensible crap, and do damn all.

I suppose psycho-analysts are the mental equivalent of Dyno-rod (ferreting around in the remnants of your old toilet-training until they reach the block etc).

PSYCHIATRISTS

There is a popular misconception that psychiatrists deal only with people who are mad or insane. This is not true at all, and most psychiatrists also see large numbers of apparently normal human people who are simply crackers, bonkers, loony, crazy, nuts, bats, cracked, blown, blasted, screaming weirdos, raving nutters, out of their tree, off the wall, out to lunch, off their trolley, out of their skull, or work for Rupert Murdoch.

However, being a psychiatrist isn't all entertainment, you know. It can be very demanding, exhausting work, sitting through endless catalogues of human misery, unhappiness, frustration, guilt and anguish. Most psychiatrists learn to cope with it by not listening. Even so, psychiatrists have three times the rate of divorce compared with other doctors, four times the rate of alcoholism compared with paediatricians, six times the suicide rate compared with librarians, three times the adultery rate compared with rabbits, five times the marriage rate compared with nuns and eleven times the hourly rate compared with pimps.

I once asked a psychiatrist what his job consisted of (this was in the early days of the NHS, before they had banned dual-personality and schizoid disorders as part of the NHS cutbacks). He said he was usually called to the ward in an emergency – if the patient was screaming and raving he pronounced them mad, if they weren't he pronounced them dead and if there were two of them he pronounced them man and wife. The dear doctor was utterly demented, of course, and eventually his behaviour was so gross and erratic that the Area Health Authority were forced to send him to what is euphemistically called 'a safe and secure environment'. In his case, it was the House of Lords.

THE DOCTOR ANSWERS YOUR QUESTIONS

Q: I believe there was a book dealing with the psychological torture of adolescent skin complaints. Do you happen to know the title?

A: *The Agony and The Eczema.*

Q: Thank you.

PAIN

The Perception of Pain

Pain is, as a great physician once put it, simply Nature's way of telling you you're a National Health patient. Perhaps the most surprising thing about pain is that it can actually be useful (other than to purveyors of it like the Spanish inquisition, etc). By which I mean that occasional bursts of irritating pain are actually nature's method of protecting the body from doing serious damage to itself – like the biological equivalent of the parliamentary Opposition really. And in support of this theory we note that the ability to perceive pain is shared only by the higher orders of animals; those that have evolved a sufficiently sophisticated nervous system. The lower orders of animals, as it were, don't have 'enough brain' to feel pain; for example, amoebae, greenfly, Bo Derek and so on.

As my earlier researches have already shown (Buckman R., *Out of Practice*, 1978, pp. 112–106, Hebrew Edition), during the process of evolution many dinosaurs evolved two brains, one at the head end and one at the tail end, each of which was capable of perceiving pain. This meant that in an emergency dinosaurs could not distinguish migraine from haemorrhoids. Of course, dinosaurs were merely an irrelevant cul-de-sac on the broad highway leading towards Man, but to this very day there are many men still in existence who can't tell their migraine from their haemorrhoids, although – because of the importance of pain in the grand scheme of things – most of them have ended up in the Opposition where it doesn't matter.

And to emphasise further how important pain is, there are actually two sets of nerves in the body dedicated solely to carrying pain messages – firstly, there are thin myelinated fibres that transmit pain very quickly e.g. from toe to brain. And then there is a set of thicker greyish non-myelinated fibres that transmit pain very slowly e.g. from toe to knee, stopping at the gastrocnemius, popliteal fossa, Didcot, Charlbury, Saturdays excepted and no buffet till

Peterborough. Or, to put it another way (and hopefully a better one), it's like first and second-class post.

Thus, when you cause pain by, say, stubbing your toe (and it's worth remembering that it's always less painful to stub someone else's) the fast fibres conduct the pain up to your brain in, say, 0.2 milliseconds, and immediately initiate the classical triple reflex described by Sherrington (who was laying crazy paving while wearing sandals at the time). As you know, the triple reflex consists of (a) reflex elevation of the affected part (b) reflex retraction of the elevated part and (c) reflex verbalisation of multiple expletives (including those specific for Mrs Sherrington). Thus, the part of the whole business involving fast fibres may be over in less than two seconds, whereas the pain impulses carried by the slow fibres arrive much later, sometimes as late as the following Tuesday by which time you might be doing something different. Perhaps even involving Mrs Sherrington. Scientists have no idea why these slower 'too late' fibres should give, as it were, a totally gratuitous burst of pain long after the event, which serves no useful protective function, but recent evidence from zoologists has shown that these slower 'punishment' fibres first evolved under a Conservative government.

Anxiety

A recent poll designed to examine current thinking on anxiety showed that 55% of psychologists believe that anxiety is a form of reaction to stress. On the other hand, 35% of them believed that stress was a form of reaction to anxiety, while 7% believed that the centre of the earth was made of cherry nougat, 2% believed that Ursula Andress is the new Messiah and 1% would vote Conservative if there was a general election tomorrow. Be that as it may, there is no doubt that anxiety is something we all recognise in ourselves and many of the effects that we observe are attributable to the stress hormones (see above, if you don't find it too worrying to read things twice). In fact, the famous 'butterflies in the stomach' are due to the way adrenalin affects the gut – it diverts the much needed blood supply away from gut and bowel and towards muscles e.g. for running. It also increases gut-emptying and relaxes certain sphincters and it comes as little of a surprise to learn that Australians do not have a word for anxiety but call any event that causes alarm a 'trouser-filler'. It is for this reason that in Australia there are no psychiatrists at all, but there are very many psychotherapeutically-trained dry-cleaners.

However, the main point about anxiety is that it has two distinct components. Firstly, there is the psychic component, e.g. a loose tiger, Oxford Street (especially if approaching it from above, having fallen off the roof of Selfridge's), dentists, the results of the pregnancy test, or any combination of these (e.g. dentist's pregnant tiger in Selfridge's). The second component of anxiety is the somatic one, that is, the effects of the anxiety on your own particular body (see *butterflies* above and *dry-cleaning* below). Now, the important thing is that the somatic component can, of itself, become a cause of anxiety i.e. a psychic component in its own right, so that some people develop anxiety over the possibility that they will develop symptoms of anxiety. Psychiatrists have a special term for a person like this and will say that such a person, exhibiting morbid pre-anxiety, is behaving like a 'fat-head'.

Nevertheless, there are many kinds of therapy that can usefully be directed at anxiety, including drugs, although there are some people who are so anxiety-ridden that they are actually anxious their anxiety will become so bad it will require drugs. The treatment of these patients is problematical. Some psychiatrists try goal-directed abreaction (= threats), others try positive reinforcement (= bribery), while some use logistical re-orientation (= pleading), whilst still others point out that for many of these patients suicide often solves more problems than it creates, despite its generally rather negative health-impact image in the lay press.

Fear

There is a fine line dividing fear from anxiety. Generally speaking we use the word 'fear' or 'fright' to describe the actual perception that we experience instantaneously in a threatening situation e.g. the M40, and we use the word 'anxiety' to describe it afterwards. Fear being more direct than anxiety, it can be produced more easily by manufactured artefacts, including horror or 'chiller' movies e.g. *Bolero*. In fact, old hands in the horror-movie business know that you can produce fear very easily by using some well-known tricks or devices, including showing the producers the budget for special effects. However, man is not the only animal that is 'fooled' by images on film. But while cats can be frightened by films of dogs, and deer can be frightened by films of lions, only man is so clever that he can learn to become frightened by apparently bland images e.g. tapeworms, plague viruses, Caspar Weinberger: also, alone among the 'film-sensitive' species, man is the only one that pays for his own ticket.

A lot is said about 'the smell of fear'. Personally, I think that the less said about it the better (see *dry-cleaning* above). Other aspects of fear include showing the whites of the eyes and dilating the pupils. These need to be clearly distinguished from beating the whites of the eggs and molesting the pupils, both of which may cause fear, or at least a heavy fine. Finally, there was a very famous general, whose name escapes me at present, but he said to his troops just as they were about to go into battle against an Awesome and Mighty Enemy: 'Men, we have nothing to fear but Fear itself.' He was lying.

MASS HYSTERIA

Mass hysteria is certainly not unique to human beings – many lower life-forms exhibit identical behaviour patterns e.g. lemmings, red ants and newspaper journalists. Mass hysteria can best be defined as the situation that occurs when individual behavioural traits are subjugated to the overall behavioural trends of the herd, flock or pack. A general election is a good example.

The central principle of mass hysteria is the way that the individual responds to certain kinds of signals, which are of positive survival value to the entire species. The classic example is, of course, the white 'scut', or tail, of a cottontail rabbit or bunny, a signal which causes instantaneous 'flight' responses, including rapid pulse, constricted pupils and diarrhoea. Personally, I get the same feelings myself in a Playboy Club, though it may not be the scuts that do it, but the price of the drinks.

In any event, responses which result in this kind of mass retreat and evacuation are rather more analogous to human panic than mass hysteria, but the mechanism is similar. It is interesting to note that during evolution, human beings have refined the signals to which they respond en masse – so that after millions of years we are able to panic at very subtle biophysiological signals e.g. news of the sun cooling down, holes in the ozone layer, the Russians being friendly, the threat of a hoola-hoop revival etc.

The true essence of the group response is what we scientists call 'arousal'. Now, in scientific usage, the word 'arousal' doesn't mean the same as when used in common parlance, i.e. by plebs and devotees of page three. When used by scientists 'arousal' means something more precise and, usually, more expensive and more fun e.g. *Lui* magazine or Sigorney Weaver. It also implies a lowering of sense-data thresholds so that an aroused subject, by definition, is more sensitive and acutely aware of incoming stimuli e.g. incoming visual or auditory stimuli that may indicate danger, such as an incoming husband or an incoming phone bill.

In summary, therefore, what is required for mass hysteria is an aroused population (of which there are a few in Europe) and a socially acceptable way of behaving in a bizarre or totally bonkers fashion (of which there are thousands in Europe). Examples include St Vitus's dance, witch-hunting, tarantellas and skateboards. In each of these cases, the individuals with the lowest thresholds for going bonkers respond to cues which, in primaeval times, would have helped the survival of the species. (Though quite how Neanderthal man's survival was helped by skateboards etc. I don't know.

Anyway, let us look at a few examples – and any others I can think of before bed-time.

St Vitus's Dance and Other Mediaeval Chart-Toppers

St Vitus's dance is the name applied to an epidemic of writhing rhythmic movements that swept through France in the thirteenth, or some other mediaeval, century. It was widely believed until recently that most of this was due to poisoning by ergot of rye (aka ergotism). Well, it was fairly widely believed by me, anyway.

However, we now know (because we now have bought the second edition of the *Boys' & Girls' Pictorial Dictionary of Mediaeval Neurological Diseases*) that ergotism doesn't really cause writhing movements and that some cases were probably a complication of rheumatic fever. The rest of the cases were mass hysteria. In other words, while ergotism doesn't cause bonkers behaviour, being French does – or being French and mediaeval did, anyway.

Similar explanations exist for the tarantella – a manic energetic dance performed by entire villages in Sicily when one person was bitten by a tarantula. Although recent evidence, unearthed by the distinguished musicotoxicologist Sir Arthur Triumph-Herald, suggests that the village would only celebrate en masse when the tarantula's victim was the local estate agent or pimp.

It has also been suggested that during the Black Death, or bubonic plague, up to one third of the victims had mass hysteria and not plague at all – though where those people are now, and what they've been doing since, is still a mystery.

Modern Mass Hysteria

Nowadays, social behaviour patterns make it unacceptable to indulge in writhing and contorting movements in the streets, except under certain mitigating circumstances (e.g. wearing a Sony Walkman). Also, hunting of witches and driving out of devils has been replaced by infinitely more civilised trends such as McCarthyism and hounding Gary Hart, etc. I should like to consider some of the theories explaining these phenomena, including evidence that pheromones are involved, and probably the communists as well, but I'm afraid I have to go now in order to deal with a major social problem up north. The Dagenham Girl Pipers are stampeding.

Skinology

Our skin, like the earth's atmosphere, is all around us. Except our skin has got holes in it to let in light and so on. Though of course the ozone layer has got holes in it now, perhaps they are there because the earth wants to look out . . . no that's silly. Anyway, our skin is the first physical barrier against the outside elements and serves a valuable role in the maintenance of our internal environment and as a storage place for wrinkles.

DEFENCE AGAINST THE COLD

There can be no doubt that defence against inclement weather has been a major factor in the ecological success of many lower life-forms in conditions so adverse that less tenacious organisms would

have perished, e.g. sea-lions, penguins, Glasgow Rangers, etc etc. As the renowned nineteenth-century biologist, Claude Bernard, so aptly put it, *'la fixitée du milieu intérieur est la condition de la vie libre'*, but since there weren't any subtitles in those days, nobody knew what he was talking about. Except the French, of course, but then nobody knew what *they* were talking about either, so that was that.

A mere two centuries later, however, contemporary scientists, with the aid of modern-day Rosetta stones such as Hugo's and Linguaphone, have been able to interpret this epigram as 'the fixity of the inside milieu is the condition for the life free' – taken by most biologists to mean that fixing the loft insulation reduces heating bills. Though quite how that makes your life free, nobody knows. Except, perhaps, in France, where everything they do in lofts seems to be pretty free as far as I can tell. Sorry sorry, I seem to have got bogged down completely and forgotten all my dignity. We shall start again. Sorry, commence again.

Physical Barriers Against the Cold

Physical barriers against the cold can be divided into two (although this reduces their efficiency somewhat). Firstly, there is the skin, and secondly, there are those structures which are produced by the skin or otherwise attached to it, stuck on to it, poking out of it, secreted by it, exported from it, oozing on to it, containing or not containing the produce of several countries, or in other ways related to the epidermis by affinity, birth, death, marriage or taxidermy. These latter are called the adnexae.

The adnexae include the so-called **intimate adnexae**, e.g. hair, nails, horns, fur, feathers, moustaches, glasses, false noses, the hair round your downbelows, stiletto heels, etc etc, and the **distal adnexae**, which include less intimate apparel such as hooves, mittens, galoshes, the hair on your toes, the cardigan you always had to wear when your mother felt cold, and, of course, loft insulation.

Many of the adnexal structures of the skin function in different ways and some do not function at all. Much depends on their physiological relationship with the body core, and much more depends on whether anyone finds out about it. Sorry. For example, horn and hair do not have a viable blood supply of their own. (Of course they don't, otherwise you'd bleed to death when you got your hair cut, wouldn't you? Or your horns trimmed, if you're that kind of animal – which three per cent of our readers are, according to the latest readership survey. And hello and moooo to all of you.)

Thus it can be said that the non-blood-supplied adnexae provide insulation by alteration of the physical micro-environment of the skin. For example, hair stops the wind blowing up your nose which might otherwise freeze your brain, and so on.

Even though hair has no intrinsic blood supply, the root is capable of growth and, by the attachment of the erector pili muscle, the hair can be erected (which counts for something these days), thickening the layer of stationary air over the skin, improving heat retention, and frightening off predators, particularly people trying to sell you loft insulation.

Sub-Epidermal Homeostasis, Namely Fat

Beneath the skin is *sub-epidermal adipose tissue,* commonly known (and seen) as fat, cellulite, flab, or blubber in whales (0.2 per cent of our readers and mnyyooowaaaaaah to you). Adipose tissue works by reduction of heat transfer from the very vascular structures beneath it, including the muscles, heart, giblets etc.

Despite its intrinsic blood supply, fat has a relatively low blood flow, which is why it always feels cold and looks dimply, and perhaps why it bobbles up and down when you walk, though more research is needed on this tissue.

Core Temperature and Hypothermia

By all the above-mentioned mechanisms the central portion of the human body, known as the core, can be kept warm at the expense – should conditions dictate – of the periphery, e.g. hands, toes, tips of ears, umbrella, etc. By reducing blood flow to these areas, the body reduces heat losses from these regions, which is really the same thinking behind loft insulation – that's why I always make sure that very little blood flows through my loft. Sorry.

Core temperature is not the same as temperature measured under the armpit. Thus, if a perfectly normal person gets left out in the rain for a couple of hours in his vest for some perfectly ordinary reason – such as having a row with his wife about whether he ought to wear a shirt for dinner for gawd's bloody sake and whose turn it is to clean out the grill-pan – well, then, his armpit temperature might be cold, bloody sodding freezing as a matter of fact, but his core temperature would be normal. Whereas an older person might get genuinely cold and you'd need to check the temperature with a thermometer placed, by duly authorised personnel, in the designated mucosal contact, oh, to hell with this, up the bum.

Yes. And the only time I did that on a sleeping (?comatose) elderly person was when I was a medical student and the (comatose?) elderly person woke up sharply and asked what the – expletive deleted – I was doing and I said I was measuring the temperature up his backside and he said he didn't think it was any bloody concern of mine, unless I was thinking of spending my summer holiday there and he'd already rented it, so tough luck.

Which is when I decided to enter politics. It's the same thing, really, but just a bit less obvious and the hours are better. Thank you and have a happy winter.

THE MINISTER DEALS WITH YOUR CONCERNS ABOUT FIJI

Q: Is it true that in Fiji the mosquitoes can give you malaria, dengue fever and Aids?

A: No, they all practise safe sex.

WRINKLES

What They Are

Wrinkles are primarily caused by a redundancy in the epidermis, associated with loss of elastic recoil and reduced adaptation to decreased surface area.

To put it another way, wrinkles are nature's way of telling you that you have got too much skin. Although that may sound slightly complicated, in practice, it is even more complicated.

Imagine, for example, a child's toy balloon. Oh, go on, imagine it for goodness' sake. You've got nothing better to do right now. That's better, and *do* stop scowling – it'll give you even more wrinkles. Right.

Now, when the balloon is young and full of air, the skin of the balloon is held tight and firm by the pressure within. The resulting tension keeps it free of wrinkles. If, however, air begins to seep from the balloon, as it gets older, the pressure falls and the once-taut skin loses its tension and forms ridges and wrinkles as it tries to reduce its surface area.

Of course, the analogy is far from perfect. For instance, few people have heads that are full of air which has begun to leak out, although I have my suspicions about President Reagan who is *incredibly* wrinkled *and* they never photograph the back of his head, which might be from where all the air is leaking out.

Furthermore, the bones of the skull (on the front of which the face is often situated) are particularly resistant to shrinkage. At this time of year, after wassailing, there is a tendency to wake up feeling as if one's head has shrunk to the size, colour and consistency of a Californian raisin. But despite that subjective feeling, it usually hasn't. It therefore seems likely that facial wrinkles are not simply due to shrinkage of the head.

Not at all, in fact. Most wrinkles are simply due to loss of elastic fibres in the dermal layers of the skin which normally pull the other bits of it (e.g. nose, ears, jowls) upwards and together. So, with increasing age, the facial features slip downwards towards the chest and abdomen, which in turn, taking fright at the imminent invasion, pursue their own southward migration towards the haven of the knees.

This slow and majestic downward movement of all that man holds dear is often visible among tanned and pickled millionaires on the Riviera and is known as the 'Continental drift'.

What Can Be Done

Speaking as a famous television personality through a face familiar to millions, I have to say that my facial features are, to some extent, my passport (they stopped me getting into Rumania, for instance). It has been said that my face has wrinkles in places in which other faces don't even have places.

There is an explanation which – uncanny and incredible as it may seem – I should like to share with you, if you have a moment. In my attic, I have a portrait of myself painted when I was seventeen years old. To this very day, I appear in that picture to be as young as I was *on the day that it was painted*! I tell you that the portrait has not changed *one bit*, despite the fact that it goes out every night getting blind drunk and taking drugs and has committed every sin imaginable from adultery to illegal fishing by way of bestiality, insider trading and standing for parliament.

Day by day, and year by year, it is my face which bears the scars of the portrait's sin-filled existence. The record and testament of the portrait's indulgence is writ large upon the pages of my face. I wouldn't mind that much, except the painting keeps on using my American Express card and won't give me any of its best phone numbers.

But that is my problem and not yours.

Retinoic Acid – New Hope?

Does retinoic acid offer new hope for the wrinkly face?

No, it doesn't.

Retinoic acid is a derivative of vitamin A, found in certain roadside plants, and was originally shown to reduce the wrinkles in hedgehog-skin, particularly when applied by a steam-roller or fast car.

In man, when it is applied to the face as an ointment four times daily, retinoic acid removes small wrinkles and leaves them on the side of the ointment-jar, which gradually begins to look like a greasy prune. This makes you feel even more ill in the morning than you did when you had wrinkles.

On the whole, I prefer the easier tactic of saying that I am actually 57 years old, whereupon everyone agrees I look absolutely incredible for my age.

Which, in some respects, is true.

THE DOCTOR KNOWS THE ANSWER

Q: My wife and I are a little worried about our son. He is a first-generation Chelsea Yuppy and tells us that he has recently joined a quasi-religious sect. Members of this sect apparently live entirely on Italian pasta, mostly *spaghetti carbonara* and *fusilli alfredo*. They eschew BMWs but all possess Braun pasta-makers and believe that roast beef is the work of the devil. Who are these people and what can be done about them?

A: These people are known as Pastafarians. It is said that they will not attack you in daylight if you keep your mouth constantly filled with garlic bread and wear a cross made of bread-sticks in your underpants.

Businessology

Hello businessmen everywhere and welcome to the only section of this book that's written EXCLUSIVELY FOR YOU! Yes, that's right – this part of the book is JUST FOR YOU!

Let's be honest – there are times when every businessman feels that there are no new jokes in the world. You've felt like that once or twice, haven't you? Of course you have! And so have we! Oh yes we have!! And that's why we at MEDICINE BALLS (CAYMAN ISLANDS) 1986 Ltd decided to DO SOMETHING ABOUT IT! The result is the most exciting and innovative – yet reliable and trustworthy – HUMOUR VENTURE since WELSH NATIONALISM! As revolutionary and inventive as THE CURATE'S EGG, as productive and solid in performance as THE DAY AUNT MARTHA CAUGHT HER WHATSITS IN THE MANGLE.

And no wonder! When ordinary comic writers sit down to think of jokes, they just scratch their heads until something THEY THINK is funny falls out on to the page. Ridiculous, but true! We know that's no way to run a business, AND SO DO YOU! After all, jokes are just words, aren't they? Of course they are. So what we at MEDICINE BALLS (BERMUDA) 1988 PLC have done is to analyse every WORD ever spoken by JOHN D. ROCKEFELLER, ARI ONASSIS, PAUL GETTY, NUBAR GULBENKIAN, NIGEL REES LTD, GYLES BRANDRETH WORLDWIDE and many other solid and reputable masters of mirth-marketing. Then we simply got to work using our high-speed huge-capacity WANGS – and the rest is history. But history rewritten to reflect modern times and blend with any décor.

Now, you too can PARTICIPATE in the

Continued . . .

phenomenal success of MEDICINE BALLS PRODUCTS – simply read the DUMMY CHAPTER below and decide which glittering FRANCHISE and MARKETING OPPORTUNITY you would like to apply for. Whether it's MEDICINE BALLS HIGH-FIBRE HEALTH T-SHIRTS, MEDICINE BALLS ANTIFUNGAL TONSIL SOAP, MEDICINE BALLS CHOLECYSTECTOMY VOUCHERS, MEDICINE BALLS-CLUB MÉDITERRANÉ HERPES TRANSPLANTS, MEDICINE BALLS CHOPPED LIVER & CHICKEN SOUP (for when all else has failed), or MEDICINE BALLS-MILITANT TENDENCY TWILIGHT HOMES FOR THE TERMINALLY POTTY – we know we have exactly the right vehicle and financing for YOUR ideas, ambitions and insatiable greed.

DON'T WASTE ANOTHER MINUTE – send money right away and join all of us here at MEDICINE BALLS (WAPPING) 1991 CO. in seeing who has the LAST LAUGH!

CONVENTIONAL BUSINESS LUNCHES

As a concerned doctor, renowned for my affirmative action on preventive health, I am often asked one simple question by businessmen at lunch – 'Would you mind paying, they don't take Diner's Club here.' (They rarely do at McDonald's, actually.) However, this is only one way in which business lunches can cause angina – many other complex physiological factors are involved.

For instance, serum low-density lipids (the nasty ones) are doubled by apparently innocuous activities such as smiling at the wine-waiter or holding the menu. Plasma triglyceride levels rise fourfold when you read the words 'rack of lamb' and rise tenfold when you eat while engaging in stressful activities such as trying to remember the name of your guest's wife/boyfriend/car/tailor/proctologist etc or trying to tell a joke which does not offend his race/religion/foreign investments/sexual orientation/addiction etc and is still funny.

In the famous London multi-centre trial (Guy's-London Heart Hospital-Savoy Grill), continuous ECG recordings showed that subclinical heart attacks were caused by taking a deep breath within two yards of zabaglione, and hypertension was caused by proffering an American Express gold card when the maître d' accepts only platinum. In that survey, of the 700 meals studied, 19% ended with coffee and petit fours being served in the Coronary Care Unit. The conclusions of the survey were that the deleterious effects of the high-calorie meals could only be offset by tremendous energy-expenditure using simultaneous exercise, but their recommendations (that the Savoy Grill should force their guests to eat while hanging by one arm from a ring on the ceiling) were not greeted warmly.

In fact, the death rate of business lunches in the States is now so high that there is a special branch of the Samaritans dedicated entirely to this problem – if you're feeling really desperate, you ring them up and they go and eat the lunch for you.

GETTING FIT FOR BUSINESS

Is there anything the average businessman can do? Well, most doctors would probably reply 'No', because if there was something the average businessman could do, he'd be doing it and wouldn't be a businessman. Nononono, just kidding. Yes, there are things you can do to fight the diseases of business. One of these is to burn off excess energy. Oil-wells do similar things, I understand, and it always seems to help. The thing is, how do you do that in the office?

Well, of course, some people play squash (I mean outside the office, e.g. on a squash court) to relax them and get rid of their stress and paranoia. But then they found that while they were out of the office relaxing, their sneaky partners were plotting against them, which increased their stress and paranoia. So now what I advise most businessmen to do is to make sure that they only play squash against their sneaky partners so at least they know where they are.

Problems of squash-playing include heart attacks, precipitation of asthma, line-disputes and split balls. Personally, I prefer isometrics. Isometrics is based on the idea that most muscles are grouped in pairs – one pulling a limb one way, the other pulling it the opposite way. The theory is that if you contract one muscle as hard as possible against equal and opposite strength from its antagonist (like in a marriage) both muscles get stronger. So you do lots of exercises like holding a piece of paper between your hands and trying as hard as possible to tear it up, while simultaneously trying as hard as possible not to tear it up.

I tried it for only two weeks and soon built up a set of rippling, bulging, virile pieces of paper. The other great advantage of isometrics is that you can con your colleagues. Once you've been seen doing some of these bizarre exercises you can say 'just doing my isometrics' when they catch you at other things, e.g. picking your nose, scratching behind your ears, sleeping, making love with your secretary etc etc.

Now, a word about exercise aids. There are two ends to the exercise aids spectrum. The up-market end is a steel-plated padded bench with weights, rollers, press-up bars, pedals and handles closing about $999. Most people develop two inches of biceps just getting it out of the box, which is good. The down-market end is the kind that promises an Exercise Programme which you take at your own pace and you can do anywhere and costs $5.99. I am over eighteen.

When it eventually arrives it usually consists of a piece of string which you tie to a door-handle and then do silly things at the end of. Personally, if you're really interested in growth and development, I'd recommend you to buy some shares in the guys who sell the string for $5.99. Only hurry, because they may not live long – they have a lot of business lunches and they clearly don't believe in exercise.

THE DOCTOR ANSWERS YOUR QUESTIONS

Q: I am a major stockholder in five multi-national reinsurance cartels facing stress in an acutely capital-intensive diversification programme. During a take-over bid, I developed central chest pain going up into my jaw and down into my left hand. What should I do?

A: Medically speaking, this is an emergency. You should immediately renegotiate all medium-term securities into a commodities or futures market (copper or cocoa would be good, but coffee might raise your blood pressure) then transfer-price all your Voting A shares into an offshore trust with guaranteed dividends, double your own with-profits life insurance and phone for an ambulance.

POWER SNACKING IN THE 80s

There's another new fad sweeping through America. This one is based on the idea that your mood and your emotions can be reliably and predictably altered by eating different foods, e.g. chocolate makes you snappy, salad makes you placid, fish makes you think (particularly if you have to pay for it), zabaglione makes you amorous and alfalfa makes you something else. Flatulent, possibly.

Anyway, it seems to have escaped the Americans that there is not a shred of evidence to support this theory – perhaps because it seems to be a totally American pastime to try and force yourself to believe in any old airy-fairy, pseudo-scientific cobblers that comes along, e.g. Oliver North (a man who seems to have achieved the true American dream of becoming a never-will-be even before he'd properly established himself as a has-been).

In any event, this whole scatter-brained shemozzle has led to the concept of what is now called 'Power Snacking'. So what's happening all over Corporation America is that Pushy Young Things are putting on their Power Suits, fluffing up their Power Haircuts (and Power Secretaries) and indulging in Power Lunches and Power Snacks. (I'm told that the fatheads who make a bish of the whole thing and end up losing their contract/deal/job/virginity/trousers or whatever are known in the biz as Power Failures.)

Anyway, it's quite a hazardous undertaking, this Power Feeding, and I feel I ought to point out to anyone wishing to try it that there are Power Hazards accompanying a tense, psychologically-threatening, low-fibre diet (including Power Ulcers, Power Belching, Power Fat, Power Coronaries, Power Haemorrhoids aka Power Piles, etc).

Having said all that, it is clear to me that the one certain thing about Power Snacking is that there's money in it for doctors who are prepared to sacrifice truth and integrity to promote it (and themselves). As one who has always upheld the nobler values of an honest life unless they involve loss of income, let me, therefore, present to you a few extracts from my forthcoming bestseller entitled:

POWER SNACKING FOR THE BRITISH BUSINESSMAN

Hello, British Businessperson, and welcome to the wonderful world of Power Snacking! All you have to do is to decide what you want to ACHIEVE and then EAT the RIGHT POWER SNACK to do the job! HERE'S HOW . . .

If it's ENERGY you're after, then THINK CARBOHYDRATE. Simple disaccherides give HIGH RAPID-ONSET ENERGY PEAKS, when ZING! ZAP! and ZOWIE! are what you need. Got an hour-long meeting with THAT AWKWARD CLIENT? Don't panic, just swallow a pound of jelly-babies, then follow-up with a kilogram of marshmallows, fifteen chocolate creams, six Duncan's Walnut Whips, a pint of Nesquik and a Lucozade chaser. Then you can go into that DIFFICULT MEETING knowing that IF SOMETHING STICKY COMES UP, YOU'LL BE ABLE TO HANDLE IT. Oh yes, you will!

For AGGRESSION, think PROTEIN! Need to shout at THAT DARNED SALES DIRECTOR? Just

Continued . . .

throw down forty spare-ribs and a hog's liver and COME OUT YOUR CORNER FIGHTING – IT'S IN THE BAG! Need to bawl out that slacker in INVOICING? Don't go in there mealy-mouthed and nervous: prime up with a POWER PROTEIN PICK-ME-UP – bite the head off a dog (make it a Dobermann, if you want to be really mean). And if it's just THE OFFICE BOY you want to dump on, economise with just half a pound of bully beef. Add garlic for close mouth-to-mouth fighting and sprinkle your meat with paprika, tabasco and ground-glass, if you need that CUTTING EDGE! Hotcha!

For MENTAL ALERTNESS, we are talking FATS and ESSENTIAL OILS. Need a pay rise? Need to explain the first-half figures to the MD? Need to explain THOSE lipstick stains on your underpants to someone at the old homestead? Get into OILS and TRIGLYCERIDES. Don't forget that a mere eight sardines contain the oil-equivalent of another eight sardines, so don't waste a moment! Two tins of pilchards, half a pint of Mazola and just two sips of Duckham's 20-50 and you'll be able to sell PORK SCRATCHINGS AT A BAR MITZVAH! Don't tell me it can't be done, because I've done it!

For PUSH and VERVE, you want BULK. When you've got to pack the power behind your punch and keep them coming, we're talking HIGH-FIBRE. Got a meeting with the auditor? Cram down a kilogram of All-Bran (including the Box), two tablespoons of miller's bran, two yards of loft insulation and a loofah. MAGIC! When you need OOMPH! and POW! and KAPOK!, then is the time to pack in the baked beans and the bean shoots and, of course, the kapok.

Yes, businesspersons, as the saying goes, YOU ARE WHAT YOU EAT, and in this fast and frantic world of MODERN BUSINESS, it's the simple rule of the jungle – eat or be eaten. And remember, when a cobra meets a mouse, as far as the cobra's concerned, it's JUST ANOTHER MERGER. Now THAT's Power Snacking for you!

Historyology

One of the oldest traditions in medicine is that of harping on about the oldest traditions in medicine. Traditionally, as one of the oldest to harp on about this old tradition, I have harped on about it further as I have become older and more traditional. In which tradition, I offer the following rogues' gallery of Medicine's Golden Oldies.

AESCULAPIUS

Have you ever looked at a barber's pole and wondered whether the red and white stripes have anything to do with the Greek father of all medicine, Aesculapius? You have? Well, silly old you, because they haven't. Those stripes are actually something to do with the barbers of the Middle Ages bleeding their customers, e.g. nicking their ear-lobes, charging a guinea for a packet of contraceptives, etc.

Aesculapius, on the other hand, was not a barber, never bled anyone and wouldn't have known a packet of contraceptives from a hole in the wall (which as a method of family planning was less than optimal). You see, Aesculapius started out in his medical career with a huge advantage over other medical students – his father was a god. Apollo, actually. Well, he was almost certainly his natural father anyway, and he paid his tuition fees through medical school, which is as good as a name on a birth certificate any day.

Even in those days that was the kind of thing which Selection Committees took a lot of notice of. I mean, imagine them getting his application form with 'Occupation of Father: God', plus all the other stuff about curing all diseases with a touch, raising the dead to life *and* he could probably play rugger as well. I bet they snapped him up with the briefest interview on record. *Ah, Aesculapius, come in, dear boy; I see your father is Apollo – not one of the Shaftesbury Avenue Apollos, is he? Marvellous, say hello to the old man from me; here, have a glass of sherry and meet the Dean.* Bang.

Then, once he was in, he got trained by Chiron who was the demon-surgeon and manic Mr Fix-it of ancient Greece, like a medical version of Clive Sinclair, really. And that was it. Three years of apprenticeship in the healing arts and evenings drinking retsina and chatting up nurses in the Union, summer vacs in Heaven with Dad and Mum, and then – wallop! – he qualifies as the Father of Medicine, *summa cum laude*, top in a class of one.

Dead easy, eh? Probably never had to read an ECG in his life. Never had to get up at 3 a.m. to stitch up a drunk's forehead. Never had to swot up on two dozen bronchitics for a ward-round taken by a demented Himmler with the management skills of an incontinent horse. Just cure the sick and raise the dead. Peasy!

Mind you, even in those days it wasn't all beer and skittles. Because what happened to old Aesculapius was that he got so good at curing people that Apollo got really envious (mainly because Heaven wasn't filling up fast enough). So, being a God of Affirmative Action, Apollo killed Aesculapius, his own son, with a lightning bolt. It was a tragic incident which could have been avoided if only they'd had a Mother of Social Workers before they had a Father of Medicine. Anyway, when he died, the other gods clubbed together and turned him into two snakes, which had his sacred healing powers, and they wrapped them round a sacred staff and thus created the sacred badge of the sacred British Medical Association, which is worn with pride to this very day on the sacred radiator of sacred BMWs all over the sacred West End.

And we owe it all to Aesculapius. Makes you think, doesn't it? Specially when you go to the barber's.

HIPPOCRATES

Hippocrates, on the other hand, was more than the Father of Medicine. He was the Father of Overworked Full-Time Single-Handed General Practice. He was born on the island of Cos, which is where they invented Cos lettuces and all things associated with Mediterranean salads, i.e. salmonella poisoning.

Hippocrates studied medicine in the temples of Aesculapius, where he read tablets written by patients who described the symptoms of their illnesses and what they did to recover. In this meticulous poring over raw data and recording the results, Hippocrates established the true tradition of real medicine, i.e. stealing from other people's publications.

Anyway, the point is that Hippocrates was so brilliant and so far ahead of his time that he discovered virtually every disease that we know today including gout, migraine, tennis elbow, herpes and male menopause. He wrote several books of which the most famous is his **Aphorisms**, which contained his best one-liners, e.g. *feed a cold starve a fever, ne'er cast a clout etc, we all live in a yellow submarine etc, I can do it Friday if you go privately etc*.

His second book was his **Prognostics** and contained a hundred ways to tell someone they had two minutes to live, and his last one was, of course, his **Expletives**, which contained the famous Hippocratic oaths. In fact, had he lived today he would undoubtedly have published the fourth volume, the Hippocratic **Diet**. Modern doctors have shown that, if Hippocrates lived today, he would be 2,343 years old – which would be a very strong selling feature for any diet book, of course, and would almost certainly get him on to *Wogan*. So, he lived to a ripe old age, respected by his peers, revered by his patients, honoured by his government and worshipped by his pupils.

Those of us who, like myself, have made a meticulous study of the art and the science of medicine truly understand how the mantle of Hippocrates now rests on our own shoulders and seek no reward other than those he received. He got the golden crown and privileges of all of Athens. I suppose that'd be about the same as an MBE, really.

Oh well, next year perhaps.

THE DOCTOR ANSWERS YOUR QUESTIONS

Q: My first is in fat but not in hat
My second is in fart but not in fat
My third is in dead but not in dad
My fourth is in bud but not in bad
My very last letter just so you'll see
Comes up twice in DDT.
Who am I?

A: You're my third patient this morning with an identity crisis.

GALEN

My researches into the origins of medicine have led me to the surprising conclusion that many of the early pioneers of the healing art were Greek. This could have been a real problem except most of their patients were Greek as well, which probably helped a bit.

However, there is no doubt that even today modern doctors owe some of their most reliable tricks of the trade to their ancient Greek forefathers, e.g. illegible handwriting. Their places of work were pretty similar to what we NHS doctors are used to nowadays, too. I mean, look at the Parthenon, which is where Hippocrates and Aesculapius did their Out-Patients. A bloody disgrace, isn't it, and doesn't it look just like the Gynae-wing at dear old St Nissen's, except it hasn't got a heap of rusty oxygen cylinders round the back? Yes, it does. And what's more, they found a stone tablet below the Parthenon three years ago with some funny Greek writing and a drawing. When it was deciphered it said, 'Parthenon Phase I – New Wing Will Open Spring 395 BC'.

No wonder, in sheer desperation, Hippocrates did himself in, or was that Socrates? Anyway one of them did it, and those were the days when the only drug you could get on the National Health was the hemlock. Which simplified charges for repeat prescriptions, I

suppose – and probably shortened waiting-lists. Dammit to hell and Rottingdean, now I've got all bad-tempered and forgot what I was on about. Oh yes, old Snot-Nose Galen.

The great physician Galen, a.k.a. Claudius Galenus, a.k.a. Nick the Greek, a.k.a. 'Doc', lived in Smyrna in the second century AD, though nobody actually knew his address – security was that tight. I guess he was basically the court physician to the Roman Emperors who must have thought it was smart to have a Greek doctor. So Galen used to hang around treating bigwig patients like Marcus Aurelius, Sinusitis Septicus, Carbunculus the Lesser, Marcus Mucus and similar hangers-on.

And didn't our little Claud do well? Only wrote 83 thumping great volumes of practical medicine, that's all. In those 83 books, he described the ins and outs of absolutely every common medical condition, e.g. haemorrhoids. And in setting all those symptoms and signs down in systematic order and at great length, handed down to generations of us medical students the art of recognising incipient disease states, e.g. diarrhoea the night before Finals. I mean, I don't think I've even read 83 medical books in my whole life. Which may be why I've never made it to be Court Physician, despite my PhD thesis on Catabolic Disorders of the Tudor Royalty and Associated Conditions. (Original title: Diseases Caught at Court.)

Anyway, Galen made it and I never have because he had the discipline, the foresight and the style. And, of course, the Greek.

PASTEUR

Pasteur was very similar to Galen in that he was a great illustrious pioneer of the science of medicine who was simultaneously an incomprehensible foreigner with bad handwriting. Pasteur's name is even today on the lips of schoolchildren all over the world, since he was the inventor of school milk.

In fact, he was a brilliant scientist and keen observer of nature and it was he who had the revolutionary idea of 'vaccination'. The word comes from 'vacca', a cow, because Pasteur first used injections of milk so that the children should build antibodies against something or other, I forget what, maybe yoghourt, which I think was epidemic at the time. Or maybe that was Lister, who vaccinated them with the mouthwash that to this day bears his name and which protected everybody against the virulent strain of halitosis that had, in previous years, wiped out almost one third of Europe.

There's something definitely wrong in there somewhere, but this is what happens when you try reading original research papers in French, e.g. *Lui*. Anyway, that's enough about Pasteur, and if it was actually all about Lister, then that's enough about him as well.

CRIPPEN

Hawley Crippen was another original thinker in medicine and was a pioneer of a hitherto overlooked area of field research, i.e. capital punishment. I'm afraid I'm a little blurry on the exact details but I do remember that he was the first to do something. I think it was poisoning his wife by radio-telegraph or something. Anyway, he did something unpleasant to his missus and then disposed of her body in meat-pies, I think, which is why we still have the famous 'Mr Crippen's exceedingly good pies' to this very day.

Ah, wait a minute, his wife was called Belle and Crippen was caught on board a ship insured by Lloyd's, which is why they ring the Luddite Belle there whenever anybody is hanged or lost at sea.

'DOC' HALLIDAY

The interesting thing about 'Doc' Halliday is that he wasn't a doctor at all, but was actually a dentist in Dodge City. Born simple old Doc Halliday, he studied at night school for seven years and eventually earned the pair of inverted commas that turned him into 'Doc' Halliday. Another two years and he would have got a full stop so that people would have had to call him 'Doc'. But, alas, he quit and went into a sort of private practice, i.e. drinking.

History has dealt harshly with old Halliday who, despite his lowly calling, did some respectable epidemiology on hyper-allergic sensitivities and demonstrated a common form of allergic response to metallic ions entering the body, particularly from guns.

THE DUVALIERS

It has always bothered me that a pair of fascist fatheads like Papa Doc and Baby Doc used the title Doc to try and imbue their vile regimes with an air of respectability. I mean, it's not honest. What would the world be like if everybody started doing that and prettying up their repressive organisations, such as *'La Clinique Bastille'* or 'The Lubianka General Hospital' or 'The Dreaded Tonton Macoute Ambulance Brigade'? Well, we wouldn't know where we were, would we?

On the other hand, it would also be a more honest world if certain doctors of well-known dictatorial temperament would own up and call themselves Dictator Doc Fergusson, or Tin-Pot Fascist Thompson etc. Then maybe their senior registrars could ring up the White House and get them exiled to France. I mean, we live in hope, don't we?

THE DOCTOR ANSWERS YOUR QUESTIONS

Q: My wife is going into hospital tomorrow to have a minor pelvic operation which the doctor has explained is called a 'minor pelvic operation'. What I'd like to know is when is it safe to resume, you know, safe to recommence, not to beat about the bush, you know: thing. When is it OK?

A: Well, it's difficult to set firm rules, but, as a rough guide, I'd say a gentleman would wait until the anaesthetic wore off.

Politicsology

I may as well come clean. Earlier this year it was bruited abroad that I might be interested in pursuing a career in politics. The response was dramatic. Within two days I had a message on my answering-machine offering me the post of Shadow Minister of Defence in the SDP. Unfortunately they never said *which* SDP, and they never rang back so I resigned. However, during my varied and short political career, I was groomed for High Office (a broom-cupboard up the NatWest tower). As part of my training I was subjected to a mock press conference, presumably to prepare me for the day I would meet the real mock press. Here is how I did.

What Are Your Future Plans For The National Health Service?

Our plan for the National Health Service consists of two phases. In Phase One, we would replace the out-moded and unwieldy, stodgy, old, three-tier region-district-area hierarchical structure with an entirely new, vigorous, managerial system, reporting upwards in a dynamically stable tri-level area-district-region scheme.

And What Happens To The Health Service In Phase Two Of Your Plan?

We're going to move it to Cheltenham. And repaint it.

What Are Your Plans For Dealing With Hypothermia?

We're going to ban it.

What Would Your Government Do About Monosodium Glutamate?

Privatise it.

How Do You View Deregulation?

I think this is a very personal matter. For myself, I find prune-juice and All-bran every second day works a treat.

I Was Referring To The Economic Instrument Of Deregulation – Such As Occurred In The United States Air-Travel Industry

Of course, you were. And rightly so, because this is an issue that justly deserves the scrutiny of well-informed individuals who are according it the scrutiny that it . . . justly deserves. Myself included. Deregulation is an issue that simply cannot be ignored in this country of ours. The American government – with the profligate insouciance of a latter-day Nero – failed to heed the rising cacophany of public concern over this crucial issue. And I don't need to tell you the consequences, even if I knew them. Deregulation is something that calls for the most vigilant, the most active, the most prompt and the most expeditious remedy. I think Senokot, probably.

What Would Your Party Do If Elected Tomorrow?

Sober up.

As A Doctor, Pledged To Save Life Wherever Possible, Do You See A Fundamental Contradiction In The Fact That As Future Minister Of Defence You May Be Required To Declare War On A Foreign Nation?

A contradiction? Well, yes and no. I mean, as Minister of Defence, I think that declaring war on a foreign nation is very much part of the job. I suppose I'll get used to it after a time – anyway, it's bound to be better than doing out-patients three afternoons a week. Less messy too, probably.

What Are Your Party's Plans To Shorten The Waiting-List For Elective Surgery, Particularly Haemorrhoidectomy?

We shall shortly be announcing a down-market version of the Poll Tax, provisionally titled the Pile Tax. All newly appearing or prolapsed internal haemorrhoids that thrombose on or after June 15th, 1988, will be required to be licensed annually, and the tax-disc displayed prominently at a distance no greater than three inches from the ischial tuberosity.

Provisions for policing potential evaders is still under discussion – we are considering using the staff of HM Customs and Excise who are used to this kind of work, or perhaps, Inland Waterways. Or, maybe, we'll privatise it and let the wheel-clampers move in. If successful, we intend introducing the Gall Tax for potential cholecystectomies. Next.

What Will You Do About The Health Of The Man In The Street?

You know, the waiting-rooms of this nation are full of mendicants – pleading for what, in more civilised nations, is regarded as a right. And I'm talking about the right of the man in the street to exist, to live, to be what he was born to be, and what he will always be. Our government is pledged to uphold that right – and to restore to the man in the street, his rightful place in this complex and thrusting society of ours. We will take him out of the doctor's waiting-room, out of the hospital corridor, out of the day-hospital and off the waiting-list, and put him back where he truly belongs, in the street.

What Will You Do About Prostitution And Immorality?

Try and cut down a bit. I'm not getting any younger you know.

Are The Freedoms Of This Once-Great Democracy Now Being Callously Undermined By A Dictatorial Government More Interested In The Short Term Gains Of Concealing The Defects Of A Disparate And Irresponsible Security Service Than In Measuring The Long Term Consequences For The Fundamental Role Of A Free Press In Reinforcing The Accessibility Of Ministerial Actions By The People By Whom Their Mandate Was Granted?

Yes.

On What Do You Base That Opinion?

On the facts, sir. For too long, our country has been dominated by the high-handed arbitrary decisions of power-hungry newspaper editors, randomly deciding whether the public shall be informed of the vital statistics of 18-year-old dental assistants from Epping or whether today is or is not a scorcher. Bent and, almost but not quite, broken under the yoke of decades of editorialising sullied by the sordid exchange of money for newsprint, at last the public have found their voice. Acting in accord through the well-established mechanism of a democratically bred House of Lords, the People of This Land have cried, 'Enough, no longer will we be subject to the whims and caprices of self-motivated information-brokers and mere fact-peddlers.' The men, women and children of this country have voted, sir, for a restoration of control, moderation and a sense of responsibility. By three votes to two. Next.

How Would You Describe Your Facial Appearance?

I believe that I have the sort of face that looks as if it's been slept in. Mostly by somebody else.

Describe Your Typical Sunday Morning

Same as my face. Slept in.

Where Do You Get Your Clothes?

Halford's.

Do You See Your Political Future In Terms of Mergers?

As an agile and alert politician, as well as a caring and sensitive physician, I am prepared to sacrifice self-interest and sectarianism for the sake of political advancement. Attached though I am to my fierce independent spirit, in an attempt to enhance my contact with the public I am prepared to merge with any major political body. Madonna, for instance. Or the Liberals. Or Aston Villa. It's the principle of the thing, really. That's what politics is all about, see?

Is There A Connection Between Damp Grass And Haemorrhoids?

Yes and no. It is no longer thought that you can catch haemorrhoids from sleeping on damp grass, since we now know that haemorrhoids are caused by, you should pardon me, constipation and other diseases of the West e.g. Bristol. However, since constipation can be alleviated by a high intake of cellulose and lignin, it now seems that if you have haemorrhoids you can cure them by eating lots of damp grass. But don't fall asleep on your dinner. Next.

Do Copper Bracelets Help?

There are many reports of copper bracelets helping dramatically. I have a letter here from a man who had very bad lumbago and couldn't get on to his bicycle. He then started manufacturing copper bracelets to be worn by people with rheumatism, tense nervous headaches, and excessive gullibility. He sold two million of them and now has his own osteopath who carries him out to his Rolls. He swears by copper bracelets.

Is It True You Shouldn't Watch Elephants When You're Pregnant Or Getting Pregnant?

Ahaha, the old elephants and pregnancy one! Well, this hoary old myth began in the Victorian era when it was believed that if you watched elephants while pregnant it caused your baby to have a very long nose. Or thick grey skin. Or weigh two tons and have funny teeth. Or all of the above. This is, of course, pure nonsense – and pregnant women should not be in the least worried about watching elephants.

As regards getting pregnant while watching elephants, I would advise against it since the zoo-keepers think it frightens the animals and they like to close about 6 p.m. anyway. Nor should you try and watch elephants while they're getting pregnant, or even having the cigarette afterwards, since this is extremely impolite and may frighten the gravid female or 'cow', who probably believes that her baby will be born with a small nose, pink skin, loose bowels and be a total pain in the bum for the first twenty years. Next.

Can Anyone Really Be Allergic To The Twentieth Century?

I thought we'd get the old allergic-to-the-century one eventually! No. People claiming to be allergic to the twentieth century usually have a fairly mild psychomotor rhinitis (what we sometimes term the hysterical snotty nose) and serious psychological disturbances including pathological fear of being ordinary, isolated, married etc. I firmly believe that this entire so-called 'syndrome' will disappear completely by the year 2000. Though I must admit I have put my daughter's name down to be the first woman to become allergic to the twenty-first century. I mean, you want to give your kids a head start, don't you?

What About The Hole In Ozone Layer?

The man's coming to fix it Friday, darling.

I Said The Ozone Layer, Fathead

Ah, yes, that ozone layer. Yes, it appears that we have a bit of a problem there. It seems that recent analysis shows that chlorocarbons and chlorofluorocarbons have been found in the air over Antarctica by scientists, presumably with a bucket on a long pole. It now seems certain that these emanate from propellants used in deodorants, though it can't be me because I always use the unscented ones and also crouch down and point it away from the ozone layer. Also, I use the stick kind, not the spray, so it definitely can't be me. Anyway, as a planet we seem to have two choices. Either we continue filling up the atmosphere with chlorofluorocarbons, in which case the ozone layer frizzles away and we all bake to death due to gamma rays from space. Or we strictly control the use of these substances and then asphyxiate each other with our smelly armpits. Either way, life on this planet will definitely be extinct within three decades, which could mean yet more jobs lost unless you're an undertaker.

Is It True That A Large Asteroid Is On A Collision Course With Earth?

Yes, it is. A huge asteroid – aptly named TV 1983 (ah, they don't write numbers like that any more) – has been spotted by Russian astrophysicists, who predict that it will collide with the earth in the year 2015 (also known as quarter past eight). I can't remember whether it's going to fit through the hole in the ozone layer or not.

Many ingenious methods of deterring it have been proposed, perhaps the most ingenious one calling for the entire population of earth to drive it away by spraying underarm deodorant at it all at once. Another theory suggests that no asteroid could possibly want to collide with a planet jammed to the scuppers with smelly-armpitted life-forms, so we may as well just carry on as we are.

Have You Been Messing About With My Wife?

No, she always looked like that.

Yuleology

It's good news and bad news. According to astrophysicists, this year Christmas will arrive on or about December. The good news is that the Universe may come to an end much sooner than expected. Quite how close these two events are is uncertain. I thought that I would play safe by explaining the changes in human behaviour that occur at this time of year and the health hazards of Christmas and also bung in a few tips about what to do in the event of the end of the Universe. Which at least would stop you worrying about a hang-over.

YULETIDE SPIRIT AND BRAIN CHEMISTRY

Not only is all this Christmas spirit an illusion of brain chemistry, but in a very real sense our brains are not our own. Well, mine isn't anyway. And I've spent most of my life trying to work out whose it is, and why he left it in such a mess before passing it to me. No, sorry, I mean our brains are not our own in the sense that we have very little choice about how we are going to respond to events and stimuli.

THE ORIGINS OF WINTER GATHERING

The festive season bears each and every one of us along, buoyant atop a tidal wave of social conviviality, mutual goodwill and hysterical consumerism. And yet, do we ever stop to think about why we find ourselves running along the familiar and beaten track both so fast and so 'far from the maddening crowd' (Gray)? We do not. As the mood of the times or *zeitgeist* (a German word meaning pumpernickel) envelops our personal value-systems in a flood of emotion, and as the hysterical frenzy of compulsive socialising, mass addiction and effusive exhibitions of pseudo-affability grips our entire society in the grip of its . . . erm . . . grip, do we ever stop to think about *why* we are doing this? The answer may surprise us. There isn't one. No, sorry, there is. But it'll surprise you. And me, come to that, so let's find out together.

The answer is that all vertebrate species exhibit the same behaviour in early winter (except Pharmacists and out-patient physiotherapists, of course, etc, etc). It seems to be due to subtle chemical changes in an unspectacular and easily overlooked part of the brain called the pineal gland. As the nights draw in and the ambient temperature falls (i.e. outside the duvet), the pineal gland produces a chemical which increases the number of so-called 'pleasure-receptors' in the brain. These receptors, which are known to neurophysiologists as 'so-called pleasure-receptors', increase the desire to socialise and to mingle with other members of the same species or, if none are available, with invertebrates, molluscs, pharmacists, etc, etc. This desire to mingle is called 'appetitive behaviour' by experimental psychologists (unless they're doing it themselves, in which case they call it research, or phone their lawyer and call it mistaken identity). Anyway, appetitive behaviour is now known to be a seasonal trait and since it is increased in winter is known as 'hibernially predominant' (this phrase, I am told, also means Spanish omelette or maybe Scotch broth).

Anyway, the desire to attain propinquity is a simple chemical matter and every mammal species responds to it by propinquing away as fast as possible. Squirrels mark a favourite tree-trunk with pheromones and rush up and down it pretending it's Oxford Street, and shoplift from Selfridges. Bats flock together and fly about the countryside in large numbers doing bat-versions of Christmas carols. There is even a bat equivalent of 'Good King Wenceslas', which is 'Phneep phneep phneep phnee pheephney phneep' (and if you think the words are cruddy you ought to hear the tune – fortunately, being a human, you can't). Marmosets huddle together in large groups and swap recipes. Rabbits convene in their thousands and have huge and bitter arguments about whether the family are all going to his parents or her parents for the holidays, and whether the spare room will be ready, which, since it would have to be ready for 11,000 relatives, it invariably isn't. All over the animal kingdom, animals are busy buying the equivalent of mistletoe and getting ready to do under it what they do under everything else for the rest of the year.

And it's all due to hormones – to which man, by virtue of his mammalian inheritance, is far from immune. It is, of course, possible that I have misunderstood the thrust of much of the neurophysiological research that I have just quoted, but even if it's wrong, it's a great line for the office party.

MORE YULETIDE SPIRIT

Take alcohol, for instance (don't mind if I do ahahaha). Whether or not you become jovial and socially buoyant on a half-bottle of Vladivar, or end up stripping down to your socks at 3 a.m. after draining a Party Firkin, or simply become morose after sniffing the

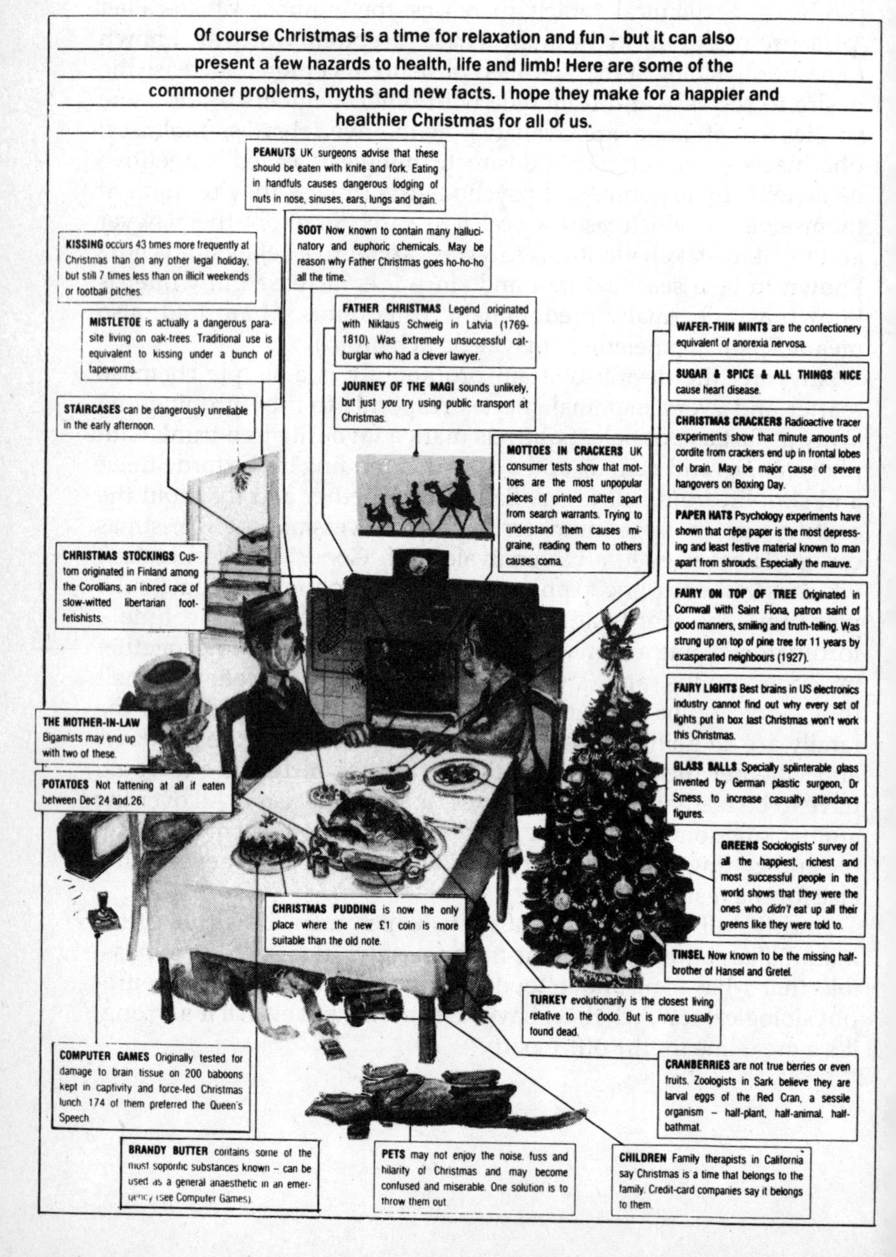

brandy butter and positively suicidal after two liqueur chocolates, IT IS NOT YOUR FAULT. It's the way your brain is built or – if you truly believe that your brain is not your own – the way the previous owner got it customised.

Either way, there is now positive proof that your attitude to Christmas says more about your genetic code than you. So it wasn't Scrooge's fault he went around going, 'Ban humbugs!' or whatever, it was simply the way his brain was lacking joviality-receptors. And if I am the kind of carefree outgoing person who has to draw my fellow-creatures into a circle of warmth and laughter around me and then buy them all a cup of Christmas cheer and then can't afford to pay for the round, IT IS NOT MY FAULT. It's my lack of money-receptors.

THE END OF THE UNIVERSE

The thing is, scientists have been estimating the bending of rays of blue light coming from the end of the universe. The scientists don't actually know the precise location of the end of the universe, but current estimates suggest that it is about four miles north of Harrogate. Anyway, blue light comes from there. I'm not quite sure why, but perhaps they sold out of red. Either way, the blue light that comes from the end of the universe is very bent – a symbol of our times, if you ask me.

The astrophysicists, who have been measuring the bending of the light, have now come to the conclusion that it is a lot more bent than they previously thought – which is also the way things usually go. Now, from the amount of bending, the scientists have been able to calculate how much the entire universe actually weighs. Although, if they had bothered to think about it for a moment or two (or even asked my opinion, as everybody else does), they could have simply weighed all the things in the universe and added them up. But that would have been too simple, wouldn't it? So they had to do it the hard way and calculate it from the bending of blue light. And the figure they got *doesn't make sense*.

It seems that the universe is overweight – yet another sign of the times. Apparently, it exerts a much greater gravitational pull than it has a right to – though you'd have thought that if you're the universe you can do what you damn well please and anyone who argues can go elsewhere (of which, outside the universe, there isn't any).

Anyway, the scientists now believe that the universe is actually full of very heavy anti-matter, which makes it appear to be less than it actually is. I have precisely the same theory about my bank account, and put forward this exciting and revolutionary idea to my branch manager. In fairness, he did accept the theoretical possibility that my account was full of a hitherto undescribed substance called anti-money, but said that I should have to pay interest on it. At least until it was fully characterised as a non-interest-bearing, sub-atomic phenomenon by The Fifth International Society Conference of Astrophysicists and Loan-sharks (FISCAL).

That is my problem, however, and nothing to do with the end of the universe, though you'd think differently if you heard my wife on the subject. Anyway the universe, now being full of anti-matter, is likely to end in a big bang and fairly soon. This, apparently, is the nature of things like universes which are full of anti-matter, so here are some Christmas tips.

THE END OF THE UNIVERSE AND YOUR CHRISTMAS

1. **Make sure you have enough alcohol.** Alcohol is an excellent sedative and muscle-relaxant for all traumatic events, particularly those involving the extinction of all physical matter as we know it. Vodka is particularly recommended since high doses seem to produce this effect by themselves.

2. **Check that your insurance premiums are paid up.** Claims are likely to be heavy, and payment will probably be delayed until new life-forms, new insurance companies, new claims forms and new currency have evolved in an alternative universe. Be prepared for delays.

3. **Eat well.** Although coronary artery disease is accelerated by mince pies and brandy butter, the chance of your developing anything before New Year's Eve is unlikely to be affected by the end of the universe, though you might have to wait longer to see the doctor.

4. **Be merry.** Not easy when facing cataclysmic catastrophes and apocalyptic doom, i.e. Christmas. And even worse if it's the end of the world. Even so, there's no point in being glum about it, is there? I mean, you may as well live as if there's no tomorrow, which one day, there won't be.

5. **Stay away from sharp objects.** Always good advice. At the first sign of the end of the world, use the proper 'Earthquake Code' and STAND IN A DOORWAY. Of course, it is fairly unlikely that when all physical matter has disintegrated, your one doorway will be left standing upright in the Eternal Void, but you never know.

6. **Keep reading this column.** I will update you on latest developments. In the meanwhile, do have a great Christmas even if it is the last one there is – in fact, particularly if it is. I shall rejoin you next year. If there is one.

Further Reading

Other Books Written by Dr Buckman

Out of Practice
Jogging from Memory
Medicine Balls

Other Books Not Written by Dr Buckman

Wuthering Heights
Gawky Park
One Hundred Years of Soliciting
Brideshead Revaccinated

Biography & Literary Criticism

Rouchefoucauld: His Writings and Spellings
Pompous & Dead – A Biography of Ruskin
Kafka's Second Cousin: Accountancy in the Wisconsin of 1920
Shakespeare and What He Could Have Learned From Me

Books You Might Enjoy More Than This One

Confessions of a Swedish Podiatrist
Ouch! An Illustrated History of Spanking
How To Service The Ford Capri 1100
Portland Cement – The First 100 Years